# The IronM Success Formula

10 Commanding Mind Principles & 50 Powerful Sales Tips to Create Unstoppable Success & ALWAYS Finish Like a Winner!

By Richard B. Greene

© Copyright 2018 Richard B. Greene

This book is copyrighted material. All rights reserved.

It is against the law to make copies of this material without obtaining specific written permission in advance from the author. No part of this publication may be reproduced, stored in a retrieval system, or transmitted in any form or by any means, electronic, mechanical photocopying, recording, or otherwise, without permission of the publisher.

ISBN 978-1986821384

My greatest appreciation to Ted Haase for asking me for my Top #50 Sales Tips – which led to this book!

# Contents

| | |
|---|---|
| What People Are Saying | 1 |
| Letter from the Author | 3 |
| The Winning Sales Formula | 8 |
| Definition of the IronMan Mind | 9 |
| The 10 Elements of an IronMan Mindset | 10 |
| The Importance of Sales Skill Building | 12 |
| Training Tip #1: Build Your Personal Brand | 14 |
| Training Tip #2: Your Personal Mission Statement | 16 |
| Training Tip #3: Ask for Testimonials | 18 |
| Training Tip #4: Use Social Media | 20 |
| Training Tip #5: Use Referral Marketing | 22 |
| Training Tip #6: Build Your Sales Funnel Daily | 24 |
| Training Tip #7: Stay in Constant Contact | 26 |
| Training Tip #8: Use CRM Software | 28 |
| Training Tip #9: Focus on the Right Activities | 30 |
| Training Tip #10: Refresh Your Sales Pitch | 32 |
| Training Tip #11: Motivate Yourself | 34 |
| Training Tip #12: Inspect What You Expect | 36 |
| Training Tip #13: Have a Personal Development Plan | 38 |
| Training Tip #14: Attend Industry Events | 40 |
| Training Tip #15: Network, Network, Network! | 42 |
| Training Tip #16: Create & Meetup or Tweetup | 44 |
| Training Tip #17: Create Your Own Media | 46 |
| Training Tip #18: Be a Student of Your Industry | 48 |

Training Tip #19: Be a Lurker and a Spy                    50
Training Tip #20: Raise Your Prices                        52
Training Tip #21: Create the Perception of Scarcity   .    54
Training Tip #22: Plan Your Day                            56
Training Tip #23: Partner or Cross Sell               .    58
Training Tip #24: Create Educational Seminars         ..   60
Training Tip #25: Know Your "Why"                          62
Training Tip #26: Follow up like a Champion                64
Training Tip #27: Put on Your Yin & Yang                   66
Training Tip #28: Create an Avatar                         68
Training Tip #29: Follow a Process                         70
Training Tip #30: Do the Difficult Things First       .    72
Training Tip #31: Do the Easy Things Last             .    74
Training Tip #32: Preplan Your Day Using Lists        .    76
Training Tip #33: Plan Your Sales Calls                    78
Training Tip #34: Watch What You Eat                       80
Training Tip #35: Listen                                   82
Training Tip #36: Practice, Practice, Practice             84
Training Tip #37: Put Out Positive Energy                  86
Training Tip #38: Use the Phone                            88
Training Tip #39: Use Non-Successes to Improve        .    90
Training Tip #40: Read a Book                              92
Training Tip #41: Do Not Multitask                         94
Training Tip #42: Be a Storyteller                         96
Training Tip #43: Be Self-Aware                            98

| | |
|---|---|
| Training Tip #44: It's Not the Economy, Stupid! | 100 |
| Training Tip #45: Early to Bed Early to Rise | 102 |
| Training Tip #46: Know the Buying Roles | 104 |
| Training Tip #47: Selling Is Not Convincing | 106 |
| Training Tip #48: Trust Trumps Skill | 108 |
| Training Tip #49: Never Accept Good | 110 |
| Training Tip #50: Get a Coach or Mentor | 112 |
| Are You an IronMan Mind Sales Professional? | 114 |
| Bonus Sales Training | 119 |
| IronMan Mind Sales Success Training Camp | 120 |
| About the Author | 122 |
| Other Book Titles by Richard B. Greene | 124 |

# What People Are Saying

"Author Richard B. Greene provides an amazing array of sales tips that you can use to further your marketing and sales programs. By following the tips outlined in *The IronMan Sales Success Formula* book, you WILL get more sales and grow your business. Richard explains why the strategy works and gives step-by-step instruction on how to easily implement the tip. I highly recommend getting this book to increase your sales and achieve success!" ~**Alicia White, Author of** *The Successful Speaker's Handbook*

"I love this book! What an easy to read book with short but very POWERFUL strategies that really will help you transform and catapult your sales! Rich hit it out of the park with this book - forget picking up all those other books on referrals, sales or marketing, just get this ONE, it walks you through so many strategies for increasing your revenues for any salesperson, entrepreneur or sales team." ~ **Katrina Sawa, Author of** *Love Yourself Successful***, Speaker and the Jumpstart Your Biz Coach with JumpstartYourMarketing.com**

"This book is worth multiple times the price. Great sales advice and getting your mind right and doing the right things. I especially liked the bonus online training. That was an unexpected surprise and contained a lot of value." ~ **Helen Justice, Retired USAF, Owner, Advanced Wellness Geriatric Care Management**

"Reading this book opened my eyes to the world of sales like never before!! We really are all in sales and the communications strategies can help anyone in business. Easy to read, well written, and laid out so you can pick out and use the ideas easily and to spur your own ideas." ~ **Andrew Smith, Esq., MBA, APM, Executive Director, John Maxwell Team, Accredited Professional Mediator, Ombudsman**

"Over the years, I have seen them all, and Rich Greene is one of the very best with his unique IronMan Mindset approach to achieving success. Rich distills a lifetime of sales experience coupled with the unique mindset that is required to compete in extreme endurance sports into 10 critical elements required for success. If you use them I will guarantee that you, too, will reach your goals. Put this book on your must-read list if you want to learn successful strategies for taking your sales or management teams to the next level." ~ **Scott Homes, Chief People Officer, Smart Wires Inc.**

"Every sales professional and sales leader should carry this book with them in their briefcase, car or suitcase. This is your one-stop guide whether you're starting a sales career, needing to get back on track, leading others or, perhaps most importantly, maintaining long-term consistency in sales. Read it and revisit it often!" ~ **Paul Romm, Regional Retirement Sales Manager, Paychex**

"Fantastic, real world tools for not only a new salesperson looking to learn but also a seasoned rep like myself. Having been in sales for 27 years, it always amazes me that there is something new to learn. Specifically around the changing landscape that is steeped in social media and new marketing and branding opportunities. Rich has nailed the tried and true fundamentals of selling along with capturing what it takes to sell in today's fast moving environment. I will be recommending this book to all of my colleagues." ~ **David Duane, Sales Director, Ultimate Software**

# Letter from the Author

As a sales professional of more than 30 years, I've seen, done, and experienced a lot in the profession of sales. If you are reading this, you're probably looking for ways to sharpen your skills and take your success to the next level. My greatest hope is that this book will give you some things to think about, try out, and implement as part of your personal success formula.

Who will benefit from this book? If you are a salesperson this book was written for you. If you are a business owner, guess what … you're in sales too! If you are a non-sales corporate executive there are tips in this book that will benefit you as well.

Most people (except sales professionals) don't consider themselves to be in sales. I think the reason is that they don't really know what sales is about. First, let me explain what it is not about. It is not about convincing or tricking someone into buying a good or service.

The reality is that people will buy when they are ready to buy. Even in those sales where "buyer's remorse" occurs the buyer was ready to buy. The problem in those situations is that the salesperson did a poor job of matching the needs, desires, and expectations of the buyer to the sale and either the sale never should have been made or the sales professional did a horrible job in pre and post sales communication. I'm talking in generalities of course because there are always exceptions.

Here's what sales is. Sales is bringing a buyer and seller together with all the right elements of information and need to create a purchase situation. Sales is about problem solving. Sales is about information sharing. Sales is about influence. Nothing more nothing less.

Everyone uses influence in their lives. We influence our kids to get them to behave the way we'd like them to behave. If you are married or have a partner, you had to influence that person to accept you as a mate. If you have a job, you had to influence the hiring person to hire you. If you are a manager in a company, you have to influence your employees to give you their best. Just telling them to give 100% never works unless you have real influence. Are you starting to get the picture? Sales is all about influence ... nothing more nothing less.

So, whatever walk of life you are in you need the same interpersonal skills that successful salespeople have to really be able to reach your maximum level of personal success. If you are someone who wants to create higher levels of success and happiness in your business life you'll find information in this book that can help you to do that.

One of the things that I've found is that the real difference between winning or losing in sales and business is **you**. Sure, product, service, price, and company reputation are all important. But, at the end of the day, the customer is buying "you", not those other things.

Company owners and managers of salespeople, don't be deluded into thinking that it is not "your people" that make you successful. If you don't believe it look around at other companies in your industry. It doesn't matter what business you are in. You'll find many examples of companies with products inferior to the competition that are at the top of the heap. In almost all cases, when you research the cause, you'll find that it is the "people" that were the major contributor to that company's success.

So is it important to continuously develop your sales influence? You bet it is! I once met a company owner who was concerned that if he spent money training his salespeople they might take that knowledge and go to another company. I asked him what he thought the biggest risk was; training them and possibly losing them or not investing in making them better, more productive salespeople and getting to keep them! At the end of the sale, it is you who makes the difference.

So how you do improve your chances of making the difference for yourself or your company? I believe that there are two important components to the sales success formula. One component is mindset and the other is skill.

This book describes both components. Inside this book you'll be exposed to 10 powerful principles that contribute to a winning mindset. You'll also receive 50 very powerful sales/marketing tips that you can choose from to integrate into your profession. Make sure that you check the "Resources" section of the book because you'll also get free access to an incredible amount of online learning materials.

Now, at this point I bet everything you can expect to get in this book is clear. But you might be wondering about the "Ironman" part. Here's the story behind that. I have a passion for high performance challenges. This passion extends to all parts of my life. I discovered extreme endurance sports through the Ironman Triathlon. I got started with this sport a little later in life than most, but it has been an exciting adventure and a wonderful avenue for self-discovery. When I was new to the sport and as a guy in my 50s, one of the observations that I made—that amazed me—was how I was able to complete an Ironman race under extreme conditions when so many other younger, stronger, and faster athletes were not successful. Compared to other athletes, I wasn't a particularly fast racer nor did I have a natural talent for any of the three sports. But like many others who succeeded at the race, I discovered that I had the "something extra" that allowed me to successfully endure and cross the finish line.

It all started the day after my very first Ironman Triathlon in Coeur d'Alene, Idaho, USA in June 2015. I had chosen this location to do my first race because of its beauty and the challenges of the course. I also expected that the weather would be pleasant and would not detract from my performance. I was right about everything except for the last part!

The day of the race there was a heat wave. At 108 degrees Fahrenheit it was the hottest day in 50 years. Twenty-one percent of the people that signed up for the race didn't show up and more than 20% of the people that started the race did not finish it. Over 500 people were taken to local hospitals due to the effects of the heat on the body.

I barely finished the race with a time of 16 hours and 34 minutes and was fortunate my body held up. The next day, at the airport, I saw another race triathlete (we all still had our number and age markings on our legs) and struck up a conversation. I asked him how it went and discovered that he quit because he was throwing up and felt he couldn't go on. I was shocked! Here's why.

He was 25 years younger than me (I was 51); he ran a faster marathon mile than me at just under 8 minutes (I was 15 minutes for that race); he was an experienced triathlete (I was brand new to the sport); and he "looked" stronger than me (I felt really beat up). I thought, *This is amazing... How could I finish and he didn't?* I realized that I had something extra, a different mindset that helped me overcome the painful challenges of the day.

This curiosity about the "something extra" led me to embark on concentrated research into the issue, which resulted in over 100 video and audio interviews with professional and amateur Ironman triathletes. What I discovered was absolutely amazing. I found that talent, strength, and youth were not enough.

I realized there was a powerful mindset these athletes used to achieve a successful outcome. I call it the *IronMan Mind* and I have incorporated this mindset into my executive coaching and training programs. This is why I believe that any book on "sales success" is not complete unless it contains information both on mindset and skills. With a focus on both of these things, your chances for sales success increase exponentially.

I'm including my 10 elements of an IronMan Mind in this book so that you'll be able to tap into the principles that will best serve you in your journey for success in life. In the next section of this book, I'll give you a quick review of each of those elements.

Here's my recommendation. Choose between 1 and 3 mindset principles that are meaningful to you and incorporate them into your life. Really make sure you have perfected how you use them before you decide to focus on additional principles. I think you'll find that the combination of mindset and skills you'll learn in this book will really make a difference to your success.

I encourage you not to make this the last book you ever read on sales skills or mindset. Sure, it is absolutely packed with great tips that you can use to supercharge your sales success, but a true sales or business professional is constantly learning and sharpening their skills.

To help you along the way, remember to check out the Resources section of this book for more trainings that you can use to continue to learn, grow, and create Unstoppable Success.

Rich Greene
The IronMan Business Coach

# The Winning Sales Formula

What's the difference between success, mediocrity and failure? Here's the secret. It's not money, it's not skill, and it's not talent. Those things are important. But without a winning mindset, an IronMan Mind, those things won't guarantee success because they can't counter any competitive challenges or obstacles that are part of every successful journey.

You need both "Skills" and "Mindset".

**The winning IronMan Sales Formula looks like this:**

**W** = Winning

**M** = Mindset

**S** = Skills

$$W = (M_1 + M_2 + M_3 \ldots M_{10}) * (S_1 + S_2 + S_3 \ldots S_{50})$$

In this book, you'll find all the elements to create that "Winning" formula.

There are **10 IronMan Mind Principles** and **50 Sales Success Skills**. The formula uses the multiplier effect of Skills and Mindset that make the winning difference. The more M's and S's you add into the equation the greater your results and achievements in business and in life.

Here's the best part. You decide which M's and S's to add into your personal sales success formula. Find those that fit your lifestyle, work ethic, and beliefs and you'll create Unstoppable Success!

# Definition of the IronMan Mind

Those athletes that have completed an Ironman Triathlon are part of an exclusive group. They represent $1/100^{th}$ of 1% of the population. Why such a small group? Because this race has been classified as the most difficult triathlon in the world. Athletes that complete this race start with a 2.4-mile swim. Then they do a 112-mile bike ride. Once they've completed those two segments within the required time period, they run a full marathon, which is 26.2 miles. The entire race is a distance of 140.6 miles (226.27 kilometers).

The one thing that every Ironman experiences, whether they are amateur or professional, is a high level of physical pain. Regardless of the level of skill or training these athletes push themselves harder than ever to achieve their desired goal. Some athletes just want to finish within the 17-hour time period and some want to achieve other finishing or winning goals. Typically this means pushing their bodies to the extreme while also dealing with harsh weather conditions, the geographical challenges of the course, and the extreme length of the race.

The one common theme that both amateur and professional Ironman finishers have is the power of their mind to overcome the challenges they face. This is called <u>The IronMan Mind</u>. Research into this mindset has revealed 10 common elements that these athletes possess to create Unstoppable Success. You, too, can use these elements to garner greater happiness and success in both your business and personal life.

Review the IronMan Mind elements that follow. Choose those that fit best to your personal situation and work to incorporate them into your life. These elements combined with the 50 powerful sales training tips you are about to learn will help to elevate you to new levels of success in your profession.

# The 10 Elements of an IronMan Mindset

### Determined

A person with an IronMan Mind never gives up. They would rather die than quit. They believe that the sacrifice of preparation always pays off and the reward is always within reach.

### Benevolent

A person with an IronMan Mind has a high level of awareness of their surrounding environment and is helpful, kind, and encouraging to others in need.

### Optimistic

A person with an IronMan Mind believes that where there is a will there is a way. They always look for ways to reap the benefit even when things are going not to plan. They smile even when things are tough.

### Insightful

A person with an IronMan Mind is able to see the big picture and realize that failure, pain, and disappointment are all part of the process. They relish struggle. They realize that life is greater than any one particular moment in time and are able to step back from a situation and make an assessment of where it fits in the grander scheme of life.

### Organized

A person with an IronMan Mind knows that a high assurance of success is based on sound planning. They use the plan as a foundation and change it as necessary. The main goal stays the same, but they modify the tactics or strategies to active success.

## Inclusive

A person with an IronMan Mind casts a wide net to achieve their goals. They bring others along on the ride for support, encouragement, and to share in the celebration of success.

## Sacrifice

A person with an IronMan Mind doesn't take shortcuts. They pay the price for success realizing that many of the rewards can be found in the journey itself.

## Focused

A person with an IronMan Mind always accomplishes what they plan to do, no matter what obstacles they are faced with. They believe that there are no hurdles on the road to success; the hurdles are the road.

## Appreciation

A person with an IronMan Mind appreciates all that they have. They enjoy the fruits of their labors but take nothing for granted.

## Courage

A person with an IronMan Mind is not without fears or doubts. But they know that these are just emotions and that the greatest battle to be fought is within themselves.

# The Importance of Sales Skill Building

The profession of sales is often misunderstood for what it really is. Many people have the image of a fast-talking, sharp-dressed shyster type who will quickly separate you from your money and then disappear to look for their next mark. Sadly, as with almost any profession, there is that small percentage of people who don't represent their profession well. Fortunately, most sales professionals are honest and not looking to rip off the customer. When at times they don't put their best foot forward, it is usually because they are lacking some type of skill that would allow them to communicate effectively with a prospect.

It is true that some people possess an extroverted personality that makes them a natural fit for the profession of sales. But that is only one very small component of what it takes to be successful in this career. Effective selling is still a skill that must be developed. Sales training can help the aspiring sales professional to develop and practice the skills they need to succeed.

Sales training is not just for the sales professional. At some point in everyone's career, even if you're not a salesperson, you're going to have to sell something. You might have to sell an idea to your boss or to your team. In fact, in order to even have gotten the job you had to sell someone on the concept that you were the right person!

Whether you are a salesperson, a business owner or just a business professional who wants to increase your influence and your success in business, ongoing personal development and skill training is a critical practice to help you achieve your goals. In the pages that follow, you'll find many powerful training tips that will increase your business skills and help you create a winning mindset.

# Training Tip #1:
# Build Your Personal Brand

People don't buy because of the product or service alone. They buy a product or service because they trust that you have their best interests in mind. They buy because they know and like you. What is it that you do well? What is your point of differentiation? The answer to that is *Your Brand*. Build a strong personal brand and prospects and customers will think of you as the "go-to person" for that talent, skill or knowledge.

Everything you do, either intentionally or not, contributes to the way others are perceiving your personal brand. Creating a strong brand makes you stand out and establishes you as a natural leader in your field. A strong personal brand can open doors and create unique opportunities that would otherwise not present themselves.

So how do you create your own brand? You need to find something that makes you stand out. Title, position, and academic degrees aren't enough anymore. They don't set you apart because many people have those things. Branding is as much about consistently delivering on your promise as it is about differentiation. You have to position yourself in unique ways in order to stand out from others.

Here are some things that you can do to create your own personal brand:

1. Publish your own book. This is the #1 brand creation strategy. It doesn't have to be a novel. Something as simple as a book on your system, your belief or even a quote book is a good way to set yourself apart from others. Even people who are not writers have used this strategy by creating a book with blank pages to be used as a notebook.

2. Find your social platform and be active in your niche. Contribute information and add value to establish yourself as an expert.
3. Collaborate with others in your channel. Look for other people that are in your industry and build collaborative relationships that are mutually beneficial and add value to your shared client or prospect.
4. Look for ways to speak publicly on your area of expertise. Demonstrate that you know what you're talking about, and answer questions in a way that serves your audience. A good strategy for getting recognition is the "giving back strategy". Offer to present a free seminar at a college or university. Gear it towards students who want to get involved in the industry and pack it full of information that they can use to succeed. You will be surprised what goodwill you will receive and the students will be great advocates as they graduate and move into your industry.
5. Write articles and participate as a speaker or panel member in industry events.
6. Create an online presence. If you are a business you should have this already. If you are a salesperson working for a company, you need to create your own "branded" website and populate it with things that define who you are as well as information that can service your customers or industry.
7. Develop your personal story. Why do you do what you do? What are you passionate about? How does your passion drive you to success in your field? Figure out how your story can help others and tell it over and over again. The power of stories cannot be underestimated in developing your brand. There's an old saying in sales; "Facts tell but stories sell."

Any one or combination of these strategies will set you apart from the rest!

# Training Tip #2: Your Personal Mission Statement

The personal mission statement goes along with your personal brand (see #1). Though mission statements have been around for a long time, Stephen R. Covey called attention to their importance in his 1989 book *The 7 Habits of Highly Successful People*. He suggested that individuals create their own mission statement beginning with the end in mind. Personal mission statements, sometimes called purpose statements, have proven to be a popular tool for high achievers. Besides being part of your brand, a personal mission statement can help you stay focused.

Writing a personal mission statement provides you with the opportunity to clarify what's important to you. A personal mission statement can help guide you in your life according to principles you establish. Creating a mission statement is not something to be rushed. You will be working to capture your goals, the image of who you'd like to be, and the principles by which you live your life. This will take careful introspection to ensure that you've been able to tap into your true desires.

There are no hard and fast rules about the mission statement. It is you who will design it. Famous sales author and trainer Tom Hopkins uses this formula:

> *The value you create + who you're creating it for + expected outcome.*

If you need help with your formula, this a great place to get started. Once you are able to complete the mission statement you can begin to live it. Review your mission statement daily and revisit it on an annual basis to ensure it still represents your brand.

Here are some steps that you can take to begin compiling your thoughts and distilling them into a personal mission statement that is actionable and fits in with the life you wish to create.

## Five Steps for Creating Your Personal Mission Statement

**Step 1: Identify Your Successes:** Set aside some time to reflect on your life. What successes have you had? What are you really good at doing? What do you do that gives you tremendous personal satisfaction? Identify and write down at least 8–10 examples of these things. Don't limit yourself to any one part of your life. Once you have your list, try to identify a common theme.

**Step 2: Identify Your Core Values:** Think about the things that are really important to you. What do you stand for? What things are non-negotiable in your life? Develop a list of attributes that you think represent the person you are or the person you wish to become. Really take the time to make a list that completely represents your thoughts and desires. Once you have your list, select the top five values and do an ordinal ranking. These are the values that you will concentrate on in your life.

**Step 3: Identify Your Contributions:** Now that you have an understanding of your core values, the things you're passionate about, and those things you do really well, try to identify where you can apply those things to make a difference in the world around you.

**Step 4: Identify Your Goals:** Reflect on the things you want to accomplish in your life. What are your priorities? Make a list of your short and long-term goals.

**Step 5: Write Your Mission Statement:** Now that you've completed the first four steps you should have a much better understanding of how you'd like to direct your life moving forward. Take that information and compile your mission statement.

# Training Tip #3: Ask for Testimonials

Hand in hand with referrals is testimonials. Testimonials are very powerful tools for helping you get the sale. One study shows that customer testimonials had the highest effectiveness rating for content marketing at 89%.

Testimonials can be helpful in three areas. The first area is building trust. A testimonial is a third party selling your product or service for you. They are telling your prospect that they had a positive experience with you and your company.

Another benefit of testimonials is believability. They are not "salesy" because they are not written in your voice. In fact, they will be written in many different voices and styles! They are unbiased accounts of how well your product or service works or how much value it has delivered. Ninety percent of people who recalled reading online reviews said that reviews influenced buying decisions.

Testimonials are also great tools to help the prospect overcome skepticism. A good testimonial has the power to convince even the toughest of prospects that your product or service can help them or deliver the value that they desire. Eighty-five percent of consumers said they read up to ten reviews before feeling that they can trust a business.

Testimonials not only help you get the sale, they also help you keep the customer. Experience with testimonials shows that once a customer has made the commitment to promote you, it becomes a part of their self-image. They become invested in your success and, because of that, they are far less likely to leave you and buy from another salesperson or company.

As with referrals (training tip #5), don't make the mistake of waiting for testimonials to happen. People are busy and they have other things on their minds, so even if they were very happy with their relationship with you, they won't think to give you a testimonial. You have to be proactive in order to get a testimonial.

What's the best way to get a testimonial? It's simple. You ask. Reach out to all of your customers on LinkedIn and ask them to provide a testimonial. Or, next time you're with your customer just ask them if they will give you a testimonial. If they say yes, try to get it right there. Better yet, pull out your phone and ask them to do a video testimonial right there on the spot.

The best testimonial is an authentic one. It doesn't need to be perfect, just genuine. Have a few different general testimonials written that you can provide to your customers to give them some ideas. Make it as easy as possible for them to do this for you.

What makes a good testimonial? Generally, one that is not too long. Two to three sentences is sufficient. Also, it should be specific about the benefit derived from your product or service. Finally, as mentioned earlier, it should be genuine and believable.

**Here are six different methods for collecting testimonials:**

1. **Website Forum:** Some companies use a web form or a web forum where customers can write and submit their testimonial either to the company or for the public.
2. **Direct Approach:** Just ask for the referral.
3. **Survey:** Sending a survey to your customers is a great way to get feedback.
4. **Company Facebook Page:** With billions of monthly active users you should have a Facebook page and ask for reviews there.
5. **LinkedIn:** Ask for reviews from your clients and they will be posted on your profile. You'll get the testimonial as the sales professional and your company will benefit as well.
6. **YouTube Reviews:** Post a video with valuable content. At the end of the video ask for a review.

# Training Tip #4: Use Social Media

Your best clients are your friends, and getting to know your clients and prospects through social media is one of the quickest paths to build friendships. This is because it's always "on" and social media is a powerful force to communicate information. Another great use for social media is to understand what people are saying about your products. This is referred to as "social listening". Used properly as part of a strategic process of building your business, social media allows you to create deeper relationships with your existing clients while also enabling you to reach out to your prospects.

If you think that using social media is a generational thing, you are wrong. Sure, millennials have a much higher adoption and usage of social medial to communicate and get information. But studies show that business-to-business (B2B) sales are significantly influenced by social media channels and smart companies are tapping into this communication channel.

A study by Accenture found that 94% of B2B buyers do some type of online research using social media prior to making a purchase. Another study by IDC found that 91% of buyers are now active in social media and 84% of senior executives use social media to justify purchase decisions. The same study also showed that 75% of B2B buyers are significantly influenced by social media.

If you are not engaged in social media you are missing a huge opportunity to market, network, and build your business and sales opportunities. It doesn't matter where you are now. If you are actively using social media to create sales opportunities, good for you. Continue to learn and refine how to use these channels. If you are not currently engaged in social media or are only doing minimal activity it's easy to get started. Just take the following steps and you're on your way!

**Step 1:** Research the best social media channels to reach your clients and prospects. If you are a business to consumer seller (B2C), Facebook is one of the top social media brands to reach your market. If you are a B2B seller, LinkedIn is one of the top social media channels you should be using. Twitter is also a powerful communication medium and has even changed the political dialogue. Decide where your efforts are best put forth and use the channels you decide are best to reach your audience.

**Step 2:** Become engaged with your audience members. Comment and "like" postings, create added value content to share, and become part of the community. Everything you do should be marketed using the personal brand you created in training tip #1. Customers and prospects are unlikely to feel as deep of an emotional connection to a brand as they feel for another person. Your goal should be to become recognized as the "go-to" expert in your field.

**Step 3:** Don't shamelessly advertise. Studies show that people that consume content on social media don't like it and they don't trust it. Studies by Forester Research show that only 8% of Europeans and 10% of Americans trust ads on social websites. Most consumers dismiss content pushed out to them by brands or companies and choose instead to view content that they find themselves.

**Step 4:** Use the two ears one mouth sale rule. It works for social media too. Be an active listener to conversations and only participate when you can support or add value. Your interactions are a form of passive selling and will eventually result in great financial and personal rewards. Be genuinely engaged in what people are interested in, have a strong stance on the topics that matter to consumers, and offer them something that they perceive as valuable.

# Training Tip #5: Use Referral Marketing

Study after study shows that "word of mouth" is the most powerful form of promoting yourself or your business. The best prospect leads come from someone that refers you. Nearly 85% of all sales are from word of mouth or referrals. Ninety percent of consumers say they trust word of mouth from their friends and family above all other forms of advertising. Also, 70% of them trust other consumers' opinions posted online.

Here's another great thing about referral marketing. It's done for you and the targeting is automatic. Your customers are going to recommend you to the people who need your services. Your message gets to the right people and usually at the time that they need your product and service.

But here's the thing; as with getting testimonials (training tip #3), it won't happen automatically. You can't just expect that referrals are going to magically appear. You need to be proactive with your customers and ask them to refer business to you. If they are delighted with the business relationship this shouldn't be a problem.

Unfortunately, that is a problem. Your customers aren't telling their friends about you. Even though 83% of satisfied customers are willing to refer products and service, only 29% actually do. If you ask they'll say yes, but it usually doesn't happen. It's not because they are telling a mistruth, it's because they are just too busy and your referral usually will take a back seat to other things that they have going on in their lives.

What's the solution? You have to actively be managing this process all of the time. If you have a budget for this, you can hire specialists that can create ongoing campaigns to secure and use referrals. That's the best-of-the-best solution, but it can get costly. Another really good approach that uses technology is to have an app that can manage the process. There are several apps that will allow you to get started quickly. Basically, you are using technology to outsource this aspect of your business.

Finally, there are a few things you can do that are not incredibly time consuming or costly. Here are a few ideas.

- Send an email with some questions. You can start by asking some simple questions about your product or service that will provide answers that you can use for testimonials. For example, "What feature of the product that you purchased have you enjoyed the most and why?" Give them a list of answers to choose from. A simple check box will do. Take it a step further by entering them into a drawing for a prize if they share their answer on social media. Most commercial email campaign managers will provide the capability for this type of survey/social share option.
- Create a shareable ad that your customers can send to their friends. Use the same concept above of reward for performance. Everyone loves an opportunity to win something!
- Develop referral partners. Referral partners are people you respect and can develop cooperative referral agreements with. You can either do it for free or for a cut of any business they may get as a result of your referral. If it is the latter, make sure you have a written agreement so that no misunderstandings occur.
- Develop your list of "non-competing" referral partners that you frequently keep in touch with. Make a goal of "giving" at least 10 referrals a month. You'll get some back… It's just good karma.

# Training Tip #6:
# Build Your Sales Funnel Daily

A sales funnel (sometimes called a sales pipeline) refers to the buying process that is used to lead prospects through when purchasing products. Even though you will market your products/services to a large number of people, only a small segment of them will contact you to find out more. Of that smaller group, only a very small fraction will turn out to be your clients.

A sales funnel is divided into several steps, which differ depending on the particular sales model you might be using. It's multi-stepped because many things must occur between the time that a prospect is aware enough to enter the funnel and the time when they take action and successfully complete a purchase.

Here is an example of steps in a sales pipeline:

1. **Initial contact:** This is your first communication with the lead.
2. **Qualification:** Here is where you'll determine that the lead is a serious potential customer and they have the ability to make the purchase.
3. **Develop solution:** This is where you collect facts and develop a value proposition.
4. **Presentation:** This is a formalization of your value proposition proposed in a presentation, demo or formal proposal.
5. **Evaluation:** This is where you address concerns and answer questions for the prospect.
6. **Negotiation:** This is the area where you will settle on price and all the other important terms and details.
7. **Close:** When the contract is signed and the purchase is made.

The image of a funnel with a wide mouth that tapers down to a small opening is a pretty good visualization of how a sales process works. Lots of prospects get poured into the funnel and as they step through the process, some will fall out and the few that go through the bottom of the funnel will become customers.

There is a correlation between the quantity of new opportunities in your pipeline each month and your ability to achieve your sales quota. Research finds that 72% of companies with less than 50 new opportunities per month didn't achieve their revenue goals. That failure rate decreased to 4% for 200 or more new opportunities. The more opportunities the better!

There are some activities you can engage in to attract more people into your funnel. It is important to use as many channels as possible to attract interest. Cold calling, internet and print advertising, direct mail, and email campaign are all good ways to go about doing this. Don't depend on just one method. You can also create content that is so appealing that they will give you their personal contact information in order to get at it.

A well-maintained sales pipeline will help level the peaks and valleys that occur in business. Managing the sales process is about creating conditions that enable a higher likelihood of success. It's about taking a process that can be unpredictable and making it predictable and forecastable. The key to keeping the sales pipeline full is to do something daily. This means every day, without exception, you are working all phases of the pipeline to move prospects through it.

Research shows that the average salesperson made far more calls in the last month of the quarter than the first two. Did they get the results they expected? Not even close. The success rate of those last-minute calls was usually much lower than any other month. The success factor is consistency. A little each day towards filling your pipeline adds up to big rewards later.

# Training Tip #7: Stay in Constant Contact

You've got the customer, now what? One of the most neglected and also one of the easiest things to do is to stay in constant communication with your customer. In order to protect your brand name, communication is critical. No news is not good news, and no contact is even worse. The moment a person becomes a customer is when they are most excited about your brand. Staying in contact with them reaffirms that they made a smart decision to trust you and buy your product/service. This constant contact also gives you immediate access to their experiences as a new user of your product and this is valuable information to be used for marketing purposes.

The reasons to stay in contact are really important. Here are just a few powerful facts to consider. It costs five times as much to attract a new customer than to keep an existing one. If you are going to utilize your time and financial resources to their maximum this is the first place you should focus. You'll also find that there are more revenue gems to be mined with your new customer.

On average, loyal customers are worth up to ten times as much as their first purchase! If you have developed a trusted relationship with your customer you'll find that there will usually be additional opportunities to bring more value to them (see tip #48). You will only have those opportunities if you have developed a relationship and communication is a key component.

Another important reason to communicate frequently with your customers is retention. If you don't know what your customer thinks of your products and what current challenges they are facing in their business, how can you be positioned to help as a trusted advisor? You might as well not even be there and your customer will notice that you weren't! Sixty-eight percent of customers "quit" or find a new supplier because of the attitude of indifference.

If you don't already have a customer outreach program in place there are some simple things you can do to create one. Make sure you have an updated list of your customers and all the pertinent information. If you're using a CRM system (see Tip #8) this will be fairly easy for you to assemble. The first step is to go through your list and create a schedule of contact for the next 12 months.

Your existing customers are a resource that should be constantly worked and reworked, over and over again. If you do this systematically, you will be astonished at how much your revenues will increase.

Look for reasons to communicate. One great method is to keep notes of your clients' important milestones such as birthdays, anniversaries or kids' graduations. Recognition of news events is another point you can contact your customer on.

Pick a tool like Google Alerts or Talkwalker and set up an alert on the person's name, company name, their industry or topics of personal interest. Then you can reconnect with something to offer: congratulations, information about new competitors, trends in the industry, etc.

Another method you can use is a survey in which you solicit their advice on your product or service. Some companies put on an annual appreciation dinner or event for their higher ticket customers where they can connect in a social setting and let them know how much their business is appreciated.

It doesn't matter if you are only responsible for selling and not in charge of servicing your customers. You made first contact and your customer will never forget that. Don't leave ongoing communication to someone else. Treat them with respect and appreciation and you'll continue to benefit!

# Training Tip #8: Use CRM Software

As fast as business moves today and with the work load that most sales professionals have, it is nearly impossible to remember everything you need to do when it comes to revenue cultivation. A customer relationship management (CRM) system can be a great help in this regard. If you are a true sales professional, you are using one daily.

CRM has been around for decades and its level of sophistication and mobility continues to increase. The software helps companies to manage and analyze customer interactions and data throughout the entire customer lifecycle. It helps to improve business relationships with customers, it keeps the customer contact up to date, assists in customer retention, and helps to drive sales growth. It is designed to assist you to improve your relationships and increase the lifetime value of a customer. The software consolidates customer information into a single database so business users can more easily access and manage it.

Using a CRM system to keep track of all the moving parts isn't just a time saver. It actually works really well! Research into the use of CRM for sales professionals shows that companies who use CRM software saw higher customer retention rates, better team attainment of quotas, and better attainment of quotas among individual sales reps.

One of the benefits of the automation of everyday tasks in completing a sale is that no small detail is forgotten or left to chance. Along with the basic details of any sale, there can be literally hundreds of smaller tasks that must be completed in order for everything to function properly. The obvious benefit of "reminders" to do the necessary tasks is the huge benefit of the time saved through planning.

A CRM system can also really pay off when it comes to gathering mission-critical information relevant to your customer. If you've recorded every interaction or communication with a customer you now have data to not only improve your products or services but also improve the quality of interaction that you have with your customer.

And that is the difference between "just doing business" and doing business that will pay big for the lifetime of the customer.

Typical CRM systems include the following:

- Customer profiles
- Internal email or integration with other systems
- File storage and content sharing
- Calendaring and task management
- Sales forecasting, pipelines, and reporting
- Integrated automated marketing systems
- Customer service systems

Probably the most important benefit of a CRM system is the significant increase of personal sales productivity measured in revenues. Research has found that sales people who use CRM can increase their revenue by a whopping 41%! Enterprise investment in CRM shows high paybacks as well. CRM gives an average of $8.71 for every $1 spent.

It's easier to sell to an existing customer than to a new one. Selling to a new customer is a greater overall investment. You want to protect that current customer. CRM has been shown to improve customer retention by as much as 27%. It will help you continue to build customer relationships and increase retention.

It doesn't matter what type or brand of CRM system you use. There are free ones and there are paid ones. If your company doesn't provide a CRM system for you, do not use that as an excuse. Do some research, try out some systems, and get your own CRM system. It's a tool that can make the difference in your sales success and your bank account.

# Training Tip #9: Focus on the Right Activities

Too many people are busy with activities that don't produce tangible results. One of the biggest challenges sales professionals face is making their day as productive as possible. Sometimes it seems like your day is so busy that when you get to the end of it, you find that you didn't accomplish any of the things you wanted to. You were busy but probably not very productive.

Despite what many say about time management, you cannot manage time. It flows like a mighty river and nothing can stop it. No dam can stop it. No technique can harness it. But there are two techniques you can use to assist with how you use the time in your day. The first is managing "the amount of time" that you spend on activities. This is what time management really is. It involves taking control over how much time you spend engaged in any planned activity. A simple ordinal ranked list with corresponding planned activity duration will take you a long way to being productive.

The second method you can use is a simple training technique used by Ironman triathletes. It is the real answer to the "time factor". It's called "**SPRINT**". One of the training tools to maximize training time used by this elite group is *High-Intensity Interval Training (HIIT)*. HIIT is when you alternate between high and low-intensity exercises with a short period of rest. For example, a short sprint up a flight of stairs followed by a walk back down is interval training. High-intensity interval training allows athletes to reduce the time spent on exercising while increasing their stamina and overall fitness levels.

You, too, can use this training technique to increase your daily productivity. Just like an Ironman triathlete, you're going to focus your attention on a small period of time and push as fast and hard as you can. People who use the SPRINT technique find that they can accomplish more in 90 minutes than the average business professional does all day long. Here are the steps to use the SPRINT technique:

1. **Schedule a 90-minute block of time on your calendar to SPRINT.** Research has found that 90 minutes is the optimal time period for focused attention on a task. At 30 minutes you've just begun to hit your stride. At the 90-minute mark your cognitive functions start to slow. This is the optimal time to break.
2. **Decide what activity you are going to work on.** You may have a project that is comprised of several activities. If that is the case, this next piece is very important; you must work on only one activity at a time. Do that one activity until you've completed it. Then, and only then, can you move on to the next activity. Don't try to multitask as this will make you less productive.
3. **Give 100% effort to the task at hand.** This means treating your SPRINT like an important appointment that is not to be interrupted. No checking email, texts or answering the phone. If you stay disciplined to these rules, you will be able to place yourself in the elite category of high productivity people.
4. **Rest and recover.** As with any athletic training, you need to give your mind a break to recover and prepare for the next SPRINT. This period should be a minimum of 15 minutes, with 30 minutes being the optimal rest period. Once you've had your rest you can go back to step one and do another 90-minute SPRINT.

Using SPRINT as a productivity tool is going to take some effort. It is a success habit that will serve you well if you can perfect how you use it. Your ability to use it effectively will move you from the category of engaging in lots of activity to actually getting things done!

# Training Tip #10: Refresh Your Sales Pitch

If you've used the same pitch over and over again and it's boring to you then your prospects will be able to read that emotion and they'll be bored! If you are directed to only use a company approved pitch then do so. But make sure you put your personality into it. There's an old saying in sales; "Facts tell but stories sell."

Get your story straight. Everyone has a story to tell. What's yours? What is it that sets you apart from all the rest? Why should your story matter to your prospect? What connection points do you have with people that make your story unique but that others can visualize themselves in? Is there something that is transformative in your story?

A good sales pitch is a series of stories strung together (see training tip #42 for more information on stories). You should have at least 8–10 stories in your repertoire that are around five minutes long. You'll have your personal story, the story about your company or product, stories about how your product/service has helped others. Ideally this last point will be a rehash of written or video testimonials that your prospect could read about.

If they've had an advance review of a testimonial you'll be telling them the background details. If they have not read or seen the testimonial they'll remember your story and, when they do see the testimonial, your rendition will reinforce the message you want to communicate. The more exposures that resonate with the customer the closer you get to the "yes" in the sale.

Never tell a story without rehearsing it well. Storytelling is an art and a really good storyteller practices. The rule of thumb for someone who considers themselves a professional is one hour of practice for each minute of the story or the presentation. That's right … five minutes equals five hours of practice!

Here are some other things to consider in your pitch. If you use PowerPoint do so sparingly. No one likes a 100 slide deck PowerPoint presentation. The goal is to have the prospect looking at you, not the slide. Use less words and more pictures. If your product/service is more technical you'll use more statistics and diagrams, but the rule is "less is better". Also, there are other presentation alternatives to PowerPoint that you should explore. They'll allow greater flexibility in integrating other forms of media and enable greater creativity. Here are a few you can look at: 1) Visme, 2) Haiku Deck, 3) Emaze, 4) Prezi, 5) Keynote, 6) Projeqt, 7) Slides, 8) Slidedog, 9) Slidebean, 10) Zoho Show.

Another method you can use is letting the audience drive the presentation. This is a different, interesting, and engaging method to make your presentation memorable. Instead of giving a linear presentation, lay out the main points and let your audience choose the topics you cover.

Engaging your audience in an interactive manner is important because the average attention span of an individual continues to decline. In fact, research shows that you might have a shorter attention span than a goldfish. A study by Microsoft Corporation found that people lose concentration after eight seconds. A goldfish has an attention span of 9 seconds!

Probably one of the most powerful success factors to a good presentation is personalizing it. Facts about the company, its performance, and its standing in the market that are integrated into the presentation will go a long way to building your credibility. A canned presentation is not as powerful as one that shows you cared enough to rescarch your prospect before you met with them. Even a fun slide that shows the personality of your prospect can go a long way. Show you are interested in them as a person but not in a creepy stalker way.

# Training Tip #11: Motivate Yourself

Let's face it, everyone needs a little motivation once in a while. Unfortunately, there is not a magic formula for self-motivation. Every individual has unique aspects of their personality that respond to motivational stimuli in a different manner. It's your job to find those motivating factors and use them.

What is motivation? Motivation is an internal process that a person develops that enables them to meet set goals and objectives. In the case of sales, it is a strong desire to make sales in a manner that meets sales goals and adds value to the customer. Motivation levels are often moderated by external influences such as fierce competition, economic factors, and customer rejection. It is a profession that contains lots of people saying, "No," in order to get to the desired, "Yes." And the ability to self-motivate to push through all of these negative circumstances is a key factor to sales success. Fortunately, regardless of outside influences, there is ample research demonstrating that salespeople can manage and influence their own levels of motivation.

Here are five powerful activities that will allow you to stay focused and motivated and enable you to keep your eye on the prize.

1. **Build a disciplined selling process:** The best salespeople don't need a boss to tell them what to do; they follow a disciplined sales process. They don't leave anything to chance with their profession. Every activity has a process. Everything from how and when to return phone calls to the steps of what to do after a sales call are part of the sales process. Adopt processes that work for others, develop your own or use the process your company has devised for you. The key is consistency in following the process.

2. **Focus on activities versus results:** Too many salespeople get caught up in the last step—signing the contract. With dollar signs in their eyes they skip right to the end. Instead, focus on

doing all of the activities that lead to the desired result. Don't skip, skimp or shortchange the process. At the end of the day, it's all about statistics. How many calls, quotes, proposals, meetings, and presentations you do factors into the equation of closing business. It doesn't matter if you are a newbie or a veteran, it's all about activity. You'll find solace in the process by realizing that the activity (including getting the "No"s is all part of what you do to get the sale.

3. **Make a plan:** Everything starts with an objective then a plan. You'll learn more about this in training tip #22. Your plan starts first with an annual one. Once you've determined that, the plan is broken down into smaller increments (quarterly, monthly, and daily). Using your plan to measure your progress and make adjustments will help you to stay focused and motivated.

4. **Stay healthy:** The sales profession can be emotionally and physically taxing. Airline travel, highway traffic, dealing with stressful situations and constantly meeting deadlines and sales goals will wear you down. It's an old adage but very true; you are what you eat. Proper diet, exercise, and the right amount of sleep are critical success components. It is very difficult to stay upbeat and motivated if you're tired, overweight, and stressed.

5. **Eliminate negative influences:** Remove yourself from negative influences or try to reduce your exposure to them. Nothing can destroy motivation faster than a negative coworker or boss. Use positive affirmations and visualization to counteract negative exposure.

These five steps will take you a long way toward increasing your motivation and inspiration levels!

# Training Tip #12: Inspect What You Expect

*"You get what you inspect, not what you expect."* ~ *Louis V. Gerstner, Jr. Chairman of the Board, IBM*

This phrase is often affiliated with managing employees. But, as a sales professional, it applies to you as well. If you expect to close X number of sales a week you need to inspect what you expect. What are you doing to take you to that goal? Are you making the prescribed number of cold calls, presentations or proposals? If not, why not? Sales is a numbers game. What about other customer activities? Are you staying in constant contact (sales skill #7)? You can't expect to increase revenues from your customer if you aren't regularly touching base and delivering value. Doing activities that lead you to the things you expect to receive.

In the beginning of your sales profession or even implementing a new skill, you'll have to do more activity. As your skills increase, you usually have a higher success ratio and the amount of things you do such as the number of cold calls you make goes down. Don't expect to make your numbers if you aren't doing the activity. Inspection doesn't just apply to your sales activities. It applies to everything you do. Inspection is an important principle of success.

Implementing a self-performance measurement system is a great way of keeping track of the progress of your planned goals. It can give you critical information about what activities you are undertaking and provide measurement points. In order to inspect, you have to plan what you will measure.

Understanding the different areas of how you are performing is valuable information by itself, but a good measurement system will also let you examine the triggers for changes in your performance. This gives you the ability to better position yourself to manage your performance proactively. One of your challenges will be to select what to measure. Your priority should be to focus on quantifiable factors that are clearly linked to the drivers of success in achieving your goals and objectives. These are known as "key performance indicators".

In order to select the best key performance indicators for measurement you should set SMART targets. SMART is an acronym for:

**S** = Specific – They need to be detailed and specific

**M** = Measurable – They need to be measurable

**A** = Actionable – They need to be things you can take action on

**R** = Realistic – They need to be things you can achieve

**T** = Time bound – You need to have a time frame set for them

Once you have set your SMART targets and have gotten into action, you'll need to begin the inspection process. Here are four steps you can take to always do the proper inspection.

1. Inspect that which is important: No matter what you are doing, you need to identify the important elements of that activity and make sure that those are what you focus on.
2. Frequently inspect: Once you know what you are going to inspect, do so with regular frequency. Make sure the metrics you are using are appropriate for the conditions.
3. Inspect your results: Inspection and measurement are only worthwhile actives if you are getting the results you desire.
4. Readjust your performance indicators: If you need to make changes in measurement guidelines do so ASAP to ensure the efficacy of the process.

# Training Tip #13: Have a Personal Development Plan

This is not to be confused with #2 (go back and look if you don't remember). The entire world's knowledge doubles every two to three years! If you aren't working on developing your own skills and knowledge to be a better professional you are not staying where you are. You are falling behind!

Start first by identifying your strengths and weaknesses and plan out what you are going to work on. If you don't know what they are, ask your boss, a friend or a significant other. They'll know!

Make a commitment to develop yourself. Let's face it, you get your car tuned up, you get the latest cell phone, you download the newest app, and you may even buy the latest styles of clothing every year to stay fashionable. But when was the last time you invested in yourself and upgraded your skill sets?

Every professional who is at the top of the game, without exception, has a personal and professional development plan. Their success didn't happen by accident. It was purposeful and it was consistent. These professionals all know that there is a trade-off between paying the price and winning the prize.

Besides just acquiring knowledge, learning new sales techniques and strategies and sharpening the skills you already have, you must also make an active decision to develop other personal skills. If you do not do this, you'll not be able to sufficiently handle the success you desire when it comes to you. Here's a vivid example of this.

It is reported that up to 70% of lottery winners go broke within the first few years of winning their prize. Why does this happen? The answer is simple. They have not developed the personal leadership skills, emotional skills, and financial skills to handle their new wealth. It is no different for your success in business. If you get it and are not prepared for it, you're not likely to keep it.

Once you've determined your areas of development, it's time to put together an annual plan to address this. Here is a list of things that you can do to move yourself along as a lifelong learner and be prepared for the success you deserve.

- Do a self-assessment to identify your strengths and weaknesses. Understanding both of these areas can help you put a development plan together to strengthen potential weaknesses.
- Use the information from your self-assessment to create your personal development plan. Your personal development plan is best developed in a manner that sets yearly, quarterly, monthly, and daily goals.
- Take personal responsibility for your own development plan. Don't make excuses or depend on others. A good way to start is to put 5% of your income aside to invest in your own personal development.
- Set aside time in each day to work on personal development. Even 30 minutes a day can create amazing incremental learning and development you will benefit from. Thirty minutes a day for an entire year is equivalent to the time spent in three college courses.
- Actively seek out learning opportunities. Decide what type and how many seminars or trainings you will attend in the next 12 months.
- Associate with others who are more accomplished than you are. You'll learn and grow by association.
- Hire a professional coach (see Training Tip #50), get a mentor or join a mastermind group. A good coach can help take you places in your career that you might not have thought possible.

# Training Tip #14: Attend Industry Events

Being active in your industry trade association can bring with it many benefits. There is power in being connected to other people who are active in your line of work, and it's a good opportunity to increase your knowledge base as well as help you to develop partnerships. The time you set aside to attend these events should be considered an investment. Here are some of the ways that investment will pay off.

Attending industry events and seminars can provide educational opportunities. It doesn't matter how experienced you are, everyone can learn new techniques and processes. The educational aspects of a conference can expose you to new ways of conducting your business and help you discover how to be more productive.

One of the benefits of attending an industry event is the ability to network with peers. Getting into collaborative situations like industry discussion panels is a great way to approach networking. In these situations, even competitors can be great sources of information regarding opportunities.

Attending industry events also enables you to meet new vendors and suppliers. It doesn't matter what industry you're in, things are changing, new products are being developed, and new companies are coming into the market. This is a great opportunity to learn about new products and services and competitive trends. Your clients are going to benefit from your knowledge and see you as the "go-to" person to find out what's going on in the industry.

It's important that you don't just attend an industry event but that you are also active in it. Being seen as someone who adds value to the industry can help you be recognized as an industry expert and build your personal brand (see training tip #1). Professionals who are engaged and actively contributing over the long term are often asked to speak at the events and to write articles for their industry publications.

And this status will create opportunities because people will trust the industry expert and they will seek you out.

One of the more recent trends is the move to have industry events online. These events typically last several days and are comprised of many different speakers. One of the benefits of online industry events is the potential to reach very large audiences across a large geographic area. Your ability to expose what you have to offer the industry is exponentially greater than a localized live event. You also have the added benefit of recording your presentation or watching recorded presentations of other industry leaders. You literally can see everything you want to see. You should participate in this type of event, but don't make it the only thing you do.

Many sales professionals falsely believe that with the advent of internet webinars, the days of the live meeting are gone. This couldn't be any further from the truth. Live meetings are more important than ever. The value that you get from a live meeting is the human-to-human connections that occur.

Online meetings are tremendous for the dissemination of important industry information and trends. What they lack that you find in live events is the serendipitous chance meetings that you can have with other attendees as well as the formal and casual networking function. More deals begin during these types of activities than in any other environment.

The other benefit of these chance meetings is the opportunity to discuss topics that are not part of the formal event agenda. Additionally, the specifics of the event and the location create a "memory anchor" that you and your prospect and customer can refer to. It's a common connection point and, after all, finding common connections goes a long way toward developing the sales relationship.

# Training Tip #15: Network, Network, Network!

You should always be networking. All of the time. You don't have to be obnoxious about it, but you should always be looking for opportunities to connect with people who can help you grow your business. Look at local meetups, chamber of commerce meetings or other groups where professionals you might want to get to know gather.

One of the best reasons for networking is to collect leads. Salespeople can never have enough leads. The quality of the lead can determine the probability of the close of the sale. Nowhere is this aspect better represented than in 1984's Pulitzer Prize winning play *Glengarry Glen Ross*.

The play is the story of four desperate Chicago real estate agents who are prepared to do anything to make a sale. One of the most famous scenes in the cinema remake deals with the Glengarry leads. The leads available for the salesmen are reported to be "for closers only." The sales manager controlled who got the leads and they would not be wasted on someone who was not a "closer". If you've seen the play or movie you will know that you never want to have to depend on someone else to give you leads. You should always be developing your own leads.

An easy way to build your lead list is to use the things you are probably doing every day as an opportunity. Here are four opportunities to build your lead list.

**The Cold Call:** Most salespeople don't like the cold call. So, if you're going to do it you might as well make the best of it. Regardless of whether you get an appointment or not, it's worth asking if the person you are talking to knows anyone else who might be interested in your product/service. There's nothing to lose, so go for it.

1. **The Current Customer:** This "ask" should be easier. If you have cultivated your relationship they should be open to helping you with referrals to build your lead list.

2. **The New Customer:** The perfect time to ask for leads is when you've just closed the deal with a new customer. They're already excited about their decision and should be very willing to help you out. Just ask if they know someone just like them who could use the same product or services that they just got.

3. **The One That Got Away:** Even if you lose a deal it doesn't mean that it's all lost. Just because your prospect chose someone else doesn't mean they are dissatisfied with you. You're likely to continue the relationship "just in case." Right? So why not ask for a referral? Maybe they'll take pity on you and give you a good one!

Outside of your everyday job activities you'll also need to network. Here are some tips to help you get started and be successful.

- Your number one goal is to meet people and to understand as much about them as you can. Do not approach this with the expectation of an immediate return.
- Be patient. It takes time to cultivate your network and build a trust relationship.
- Do not be selling! You will turn people off as they know that all you care about is yourself. People don't care about you until they know you care about them.
- Actively find ways to make connections between members of your network.

# Training Tip #16: Create & Meetup or Tweetup

Creating your own meetings is a great way to create networking opportunities (see tip #15). What if your local area is light in network group opportunities? Creating a meeting to fill the gap can be a great way to increase your personal authority and brand recognition. A tweetup is an easy thing to create. Go-getters are always looking for ways to network and if you create one you'll be the hero.

One of the best ways to assert yourself as a leader is to create a group for other people to connect. A meetup group is something more permanent where like-minded people can join and connect online or at live events. You can learn more and create your own at www.Meetup.com.

Though meetups can be virtual, the best kind of meetup is a face-to-face one. If you do a live meetup, you'll have to choose the type of venue where you will hold your meeting. Company conference rooms, libraries, restaurants, and hotel meeting rooms are some of the typical choices. You'll also want to decide what type of group it will be. Will you share content? Will it be a teaching group? Will you allow others to share the stage? What type of networking will be allowed? How often will you meet? Will there be a fee to join or monthly dues? These are just a few of the questions that you'll have to answer as you get started forming your group.

A tweetup is the same as a meetup in terms of gathering like-minded individuals together for a purpose. The biggest difference is that there is less online structure. Meetup.com provides web pages that are permanent and allow you to plan, communicate with your members, charge membership, and a whole host of other activities. Creating a tweetup is a simple case of announcing your meeting via Twitter.

If you travel a lot in your career, tweetups are a great tool to put together an impromptu gathering of people. If you are a frequent guest at the same hotel or have status at a major chain you often can use the hotel's restaurant or bar without having to reserve (pay for) a room. Just make sure to reciprocate by asking your attendees to order something and take care of the wait staff. Your Tweetup doesn't have to be at the hotel you're staying at. Just like a meetup, you can find some other satiable place that you know will work that can be the event location. Doing a tweetup is as simple as tweeting the details of your event frequently to build awareness.

Whether you decide to do a meetup or a tweetup the preparation is the same. Here is a list of activities you can focus on to get started:

- Show up early. Be the first person there and be on the alert for others who are looking for your meeting. People who show up early and find no one there often lose their nerve or think that the meeting is not going to be well attended and they leave.

- Put out signs at your location so people know where to go for the meeting.

- Bring name tags and a marker. Most people have a difficult time remembering names at first and this will make things much easier and comfortable for the meeting attendees.

- Bring small pads of paper and pens. Some people will like to take notes on their mobile device and others will want to write on physical media. You don't need to have a pad for everyone. Just a few for those who forget to bring theirs.

- Bring your business cards, marketing materials or book (see training tip #1 on branding).

- Bring your camera or camera enabled mobile device and take lots of pictures of the attendees.

- Post pictures on social media of people attending the event while the event is going on.

# Training Tip #17: Create Your Own Media

This is a really easy way to create value for clients or prospects. A newsletter, a podcast, a BLOG or a VLOG are easy ways to reach the masses, create value, and help to build your personal brand (see #1). You don't have to be a writer or movie star to do this. It can be as simple as repurposing other materials or articles (with proper citation) that exist that add value to the audience you are trying to reach.

If you are going to create your own content and message for your customers, you want to make it as easy for them to consume it as possible. Everyone has a different learning style. Some people like to read, some like to listen to audio recordings, and some like to watch videos. You should provide your content in all three mediums. That might sound like a lot of work, but if you know how to leverage your time it is a very achievable goal.

Here is the secret to maximizing your reach with your content, building a following, and building your brand. The best way to be in many places at once is to leverage your content in a manner that it is easily repurposed. Do you want to do something once and have it in three different types of media? Here's how you do it.

Set up your video camera or use your PC camera and begin to talk about the topic you want to communicate. You don't need expensive equipment or production-ready videos to get started. The secret is to get started! Video is the best place to start because people are consuming video at an ever-growing rate. It has become the preferable form of information consumption for many people over blogs and podcasts.

Once you have your recording, you can do some editing to make it presentable and then publish it on one of the many video sites available to you. Two of the big free ones with large audiences are YouTube and Vimeo. Your video file is the foundation for your podcast and your blog.

To create your blog, take the video file and either run it through voice-to-text recognition software or send it to someone for transcription. There are many transcription services available that won't charge a lot. A great place to start looking for that type of service is Fiverr.com. Once you have the transcript of your video, you can make the necessary adjustments and post it to your website or any blogging platform that you subscribe to.

The final step is to create your podcast. This is as simple as separating the audio piece from the video file that you have and creating an MP3 to post on your website or one of the many podcast platforms that exist. These simple steps will get you started and, as you become more comfortable with the process, you can begin to work on many of the elements to "dress things up". Don't worry about trying to make things perfect when you begin. Just get started!

The alternative to the aforementioned steps is to begin with the blog. If you are comfortable writing, this will appeal to you. After your blog has been completed you can read it while you are creating a video recording and use that file to create your podcast. For examples of blogs, VLOGs, and podcasts go to www.IronManMind.com.

One of the biggest obstacles for many people in getting started is that they don't like to see themselves in a video. This is because our internal perception of how we look often does not match with the external view. And for some this can be disconcerting. Get over it! People don't expect you to be smooth and polished like a newscaster. If you relax, be yourself, and don't worry about making little mistakes, you'll find that people will easily connect with who you are. You'll appear genuine and this goes a long way to building a trusted relationship with your audience.

# Training Tip #18: Be a Student of Your Industry

For one of the best reasons to always be learning you need look no further than Lewis Carroll's Through the Looking-Glass. In the book, the Red Queen said to Alice, "Now, here, you see, it takes all the running you can do, to keep in the same place." Scientists who study evolution refer to this as the Red Queen Theory, which is an evolutionary hypothesis that proposes that organisms must constantly adapt and evolve, simply to survive.

If you think about the statement the Red Queen makes, she says you must run in order to stay in the same place. What about getting ahead? To get ahead you need to be smarter and you need to move faster! Gaining knowledge is one of the best ways to do that. As a sales professional you should always be learning about what is going on in the industry and share your best knowledge with your prospects, customers, and peers.

In today's fast-paced business environment, complacency does not beget success. In the rapid high tech age, companies and jobs rise and fall in a matter of months. The entire world's knowledge doubles every two to three years. The skills you possess or the job you do could be replaced any day by a free app. Your ability to earn a living for yourself is always at risk by some form of technology.

How many times have you heard of people making drastic career changes such as accountant to yoga instructor or insurance salesperson to photographer? It happens more and more and these people are only able to succeed in this shift because they have a mindset that is flexible and motivated. A motivated self-educated individual can learn a little bit about everything or they can work hard toward mastering a single subject. In your case it's the profession of sales and the industry you work in.

One of the greatest advancements in modern day history is the commercialization of the internet. Technology has provided the opportunity for us to be excellent gatherers of information. In fact, you can almost get the equivalent of a university degree for free on the internet. The only thing missing is a degree to hang on the wall and an empty bank account. There are many free university classes, books, podcasts, blogs, and other online courses from professionals in almost any industry that you can take advantage of.

One of the challenges that some people have is a lack of discipline to engage in daily learning. It's so much easier in the evenings to binge watch Netflix! Learning is a commitment. It is an act of conscious and diligent effort. How do you become a lifelong learner? There are lots of ways. People often say that they don't have time to read a book or go to a seminar. Not having enough time is an excuse and not a very good one. There are plenty of self-help audio programs that are available, which have been put together by some of the most successful professionals in every walk of life. How hard is it to listen to an audiobook while you're driving somewhere in your car?

If you're wondering how much time you should put aside for your personal development the answer is the more the better! But all it takes is a minimum of 30 minutes each day to get started. Thirty minutes a day, every day for one year is 182 hours. A typical college course is 15 weeks of lecture and 45 hours of external study. If you spent only 30 minutes a day for an entire year, you would achieve the equivalent time spent in three college courses!

Where do you find 30 minutes? Easily the number one time drain in today's society is television. The average American watches an average of nearly 35 hours of television each week. The second is social media. Replace those hours with learning and you'll earn a life that is greatly rewarding.

# Training Tip #19: Be a Lurker and a Spy

You should know exactly what your competitors are doing. Why should your prospects know more than you? Look on competitive company websites, read press releases, product descriptions, etc. Go to GlassDoor.com and see what employees are saying about these companies. Chances are that that their reviews (good or bad) will show in their sales presentations. Know the individuals you are selling against. If they win a sale over you call them and congratulate them. Friendly competition is a good thing. Or some might say, "Keep your friends close and your enemies closer!"

Just who are your competitors? Well, obviously they are those that have a product or service that is very similar to yours. If you sell a commodity, price plays a large factor in the purchase decision making process and you probably know who those companies are. There are also other companies that you should consider as your competitors. Those companies that provide products that are ancillary to what you do are also "competing" for budgeting dollars. Even though there is no direct head-to-head competition you should know who they are, what role they play for your customer, and work to determine their value to your customer as it stacks up against yours.

Here's an example of non-competing products that compete for purchasing budgets. In the world of brick and mortar retailing, it is not uncommon for companies that have new product introductions to be prepared to recommend what products should be discontinued in order to make room on the shelves for their new products. The competition for shelf space is fierce and only the most popular, high volume or high margin products get to keep their space on the shelf. In these instances, your knowledge of your customers' business had better extend far beyond the product you are selling.

There's another good reason to monitor your competitors. Since you have already collected competitive intelligence on them, you can use that data to create defensive strategies. You can also use the information to devise offensive strategies. By monitoring your competitors on an on-going basis you get to know their behavior and you can start to anticipate what they will likely do in certain situations. This information will allow you to head off your competition and increase your wins in competitive RFPs or "bake-offs". Keeping an eye on your customers is a great strategy for growing your business.

Here are some tips to get started researching your competitors:

- Look at your competitor's website. Start by looking at what the company sells and compare it to your own products and services. Look at their unique selling proposition (USP). Do they have a position that differentiates them in a way that matters to the consumer?
- Search for a blog, VLOG or podcast. You should see how often they post and what type of content they put up.
- Check their social media. See how many "likes" or "shares" they get. This will give you some indication of how well their content resonates with customers. Start with the most popular channels: Facebook, Twitter, Instagram, Pinterest, Google Plus and YouTube.
- Check their online reputation. What have people said about them on Google, Yelp, Citysearch and other industry sites where people talk about their experiences? How do their reviews compare to yours?
- Google Alerts: Set up competitive alerts so that you get an email whenever your competitor shows up in the news.

Once you have looked at all of these variables, you can put together a complete competitive analysis and determine how you can position your business against them.

# Training Tip #20: Raise Your Prices

If you work for a company that has a pricing committee you may not be able to easily raise your prices. But if you are a business owner or have the authority to make pricing changes it is better to be seen as a premium priced, high value provider than a commodity priced seller. If you sell a commodity product move on to training tip #21, but don't forget that you can still increase your revenue opportunity with the upsell (see training tip#5).

There's an old saying (actually there are a lot of old sayings in sales) that goes something like this: When you sell on price, you rent the business. But when you sell on value, you own the business. Lowering a price is the lazy way out of the inevitable resistance to price objection. If you make price the primary deciding factor, customers who buy on price will leave you in a second as soon as they can find a lower price. What's more, if the only reason your customers buy from you is price, you or your company are irrelevant. Your skills, service, great personality or good looks mean nothing! They can go to the internet and search the lowest price.

The fact of the matter is that any price will seem too high if you haven't established a high level of value with the customer. When addressing the issue of price with the customer, you want to be able to help them look at the larger picture. What are they factoring into the cost of ownership? Is it maintenance, reliability, durability of the product, easy access to technical or mechanical support or something else?

When you look at the big picture in this manner, it's not about price, it's about cost. That's right. In the buying formula price is a moderating variable. It is at least equal to all of the other decision factors that the buyer takes into consideration. In fact, using the word "investment" instead of "price" can change the customer's perception of price to a more favorable one.

If you understand how that decision formula works, cost is a negative multiplier. And here's another kicker, cost is not always measured in currency. It could be frustration, loss of use of the product, interruption in operations or a whole host of tangentially related circumstances.

Price is what your customer will pay for the product but cost is what the customer pays if they make a decision that is wrong or can negatively impact another part of the enterprise. Before the days of planned obsolesce or cheap products made overseas, the higher cost products often equated to a better value. This can still be the case if you make sure you address the value proposition upfront. Use statistics on product longevity and the cost to maintain the product. Tell stories (see training tip #42) about benefits that referenceable customers have gotten from using your product or service. Always sell on value, not on price!

Usually, if there is no resistance to price, you may have another problem; you may be underpriced and leaving money on the table. Remember that the primary objective of a business is to maximize the value (or income) to the stockholders or owners. Underpricing what you sell does not follow the tenets of good business practices.

Here are some tips to help you increase your prices.

- Introduce the higher prices in stages to a small group of customers first to see how they react. If most of them accept it, you can expand the increase to your entire customer base.
- Keep your existing customers at the current price level but charge higher prices for new customers.
- Create a new product by bundling together a mixture of products/services that has a higher perceived value.
- Create quantity value pricing (i.e. larger quantities cost less per item).
- Add improvements to the product and charge more.

# Training Tip #21: Create the Perception of Scarcity

Like any element of the "buy" decision, there is a lot of psychology in this training tip. Scarcity is the concept of limited availability of a product or service. Buyer behavior in this type of situation demonstrates that when this limitation occurs, the product or service becomes more attractive to the consumer. From an economic point of view, the forces at work are simple—supply and demand. Where there is less supply of a desired good or service, this drives up desire, demand, and often the price of the good or service.

Think about this on a psychological level. Going all the way back to when you were a child, when you were told you couldn't have something, didn't that make you want to have it even more? Of course it did and this base desire not to miss out on something has not gone away just because you entered adulthood. The mechanisms that trigger this behavior may be a little more sophisticated, but the behavior is still there.

The concept of scarcity can manifest itself in a variety of ways. To some people, owning an item that is scarce or in limited supply promotes the feeling of exclusivity. Think about "limited production" goods like cars, jewelry or even tennis shoes. People will stand in line for hours or even days to get the opportunity to spend 10+ times the normal price to be the owner of an exclusive product. This appeals to the ego in a manner that takes the individual all the way to the top of Maslow's Hierarchy of Needs Pyramid.

Another aspect of owning a product that other people can't is the feeling of power. Belonging to a member approved club, traveling in first class seats or anything that separates the individual from the masses can be very attractive to certain people. This is because the opportunity is limited in supply and only certain people who have the economic means and purchase disposition will be driven towards this purchase opportunity. Though they are separate decision purchase elements, power and exclusivity are very closely related.

Another element of scarcity is the perception of increased value. There are a multitude of behavior studies that demonstrate that given a choice of like products, the consumer will show greater favor toward the product that has less supply. Consumers will often think that a product that has a smaller stock or supply must be more popular. It's the perception of social proof without the actual proof!

Creating the perception of scarcity takes a little work. What do you do if the good or service is not in limited supply? In these instances, you have to create marketing situations that enable a limit to the opportunity. An example might be a special discount that expires or a bonus product if the customer purchases by a certain time. No one wants to miss out on an opportunity. This is another psychological "buy" motivator called "fear of loss".

Famous psychologist, researcher, and author of countless articles on consumer behavior Daniel Kahneman has created the Loss Aversion Theory. Kahneman found that the psychological pain of losing out on something is almost twice as powerful as the pleasure of getting or gaining an opportunity. Fear of loss marketing tactics are very popular in online sales and can be seen in the "countdown clock" or the frequent emails warning of expiring discounts or limited availability.

If you are a corporate salesperson and your company does not use scarcity as a marketing tool, do not let that stop you. Create your own limited promotion. Invest in your own good, service or even event ticket that the customer or prospect gets if they purchase within a specified time period. If you are commissioned, you are investing in increasing your own income!

# Training Tip #22: Plan Your Day

This is closely related to #9 but covers your daily goals, calendaring, and strategies for handling the unexpected distractions. The top professionals in their field all plan their day in detail. Abraham Lincoln said, "If I had 8 hours to chop down a tree I'd spend 6 hours sharpening my ax." Old Abe knew that the power is in the planning.

A study by the University of Scranton shows that 84% of the population had no specific goals at all, 13% had goals but they were not committed to paper, and 3% had clear written goals and plans to accomplish them. Which percentage do you fall into? If it's the 84%, don't worry. You can change that! And NOW is the best time to do it.

One of the top reasons why so many people fail in realizing their daily goals is that their expectations are either unrealistic for the time frame they set or the strategy that they devise for goal attainment is too complicated to achieve. People create a long list of goals and think that if they just tick down the list they'll get everything done. The problem with this is that the average person has so many competing priorities that this type of approach is doomed to failure. It's better to have a shorter list and goals that are realistic for attainment with everything that is going on in your life. All you need to do to move towards higher daily productivity is take three simple steps.

**Step 1: Make a List**
The reason you want to make a list is that research shows that people who write down their daily goals have a much higher likelihood of accomplishing them. In fact, the statistics go something like this. If you make a goal and don't write it down, you have a 21% chance of successfully accomplishing that goal. If you write the goal down, that statistic rises to 72%. If you write the goal down and you tell someone about it, the probability of success goes up to a whopping 86%!

Research also shows that the most effective means of recording your daily goals is to "go old school". That means you use a pen and paper as opposed to typing it in your phone or on a PC. When you write things down, you go through a filtering process of ideas because it takes longer to write than type. The additional time and energy required to move your pen means you are more thoughtful in what you capture on the page and you are more likely to remember and be focused on achieving that activity during the day.

## Step 2: Order Your List

Once you have a list you will need to order it from most important to least important. Order of importance can be based on whatever ranking you wish to use, but you should take into account the things that are going to have the biggest positive impact on your life. Those items should be at the top of your list. It is important that your goals be measurable and that you have a timeline for accomplishing them. A goal without a deadline is nothing more than a wish. A good method for goal accomplishment is to write them on your daily calendar. Block out a time on the calendar when you do nothing except work on that goal.

## Step 3: Employ the Law of Limitations

Finally, here's the secret sauce to accomplishing everything on your list. *You purposely limit your daily task list.* This is called the Law of Limitations. You probably can't do everything you have on your list and, if you try to, you're likely to fail. Try to be realistic about the effort and time you will need to put forth to achieve your goals. This is the biggest trap that many people fall into. They get excited and overly optimistic about what they want to do.

What happens if you achieve all the goals on your list before you planned to? That's wonderful! Reap the rewards and get ready to add some new goals. Everything extra you achieve after accomplishing those first set of goals is a bonus.

# Training Tip #23: Partner or Cross Sell

Many salespeople are averse to engaging in cross-selling. Why? Because they see risk in bringing another person into the sales process. Even if there is a formal referral agreement between the two parties they don't think it is worth the risk of having someone else mess with their customer relationships.

Here's the problem with that. It's selfish! Having that attitude is all about you and not all about the customer. When the mission is to create value with cross-selling by bringing new opportunities, the customer will see the benefits and give you credit for it. The best part of this is that cross-selling is one of the most profitable and least risky endeavors a company can undertake. Better yet, research shows that most customers prefer a full line of products and services to choose from and appreciate the convenience of having an opportunity that presents a more complete solution than a "one-off" sale.

There are three different types of cross-selling. You need to decide which type fits the sales situation and then use it appropriately. You can 1) sell to an unrelated need, 2) sell sequentially upstream or downstream from a partner sale, or 3) sell an integrated solution. If you decide to take advantage of a cross-selling situation, you must ensure that it is tightly administered. All participating partners must be in full agreement as to the flow of the presentation, the objectives, and the strategies. If you do not do this you run the risk of losing customers and creating conflict within your partner cross-sell team.

One of the first steps to figure out who to partner with to create a cross-selling team is relevance. Your goal in any sales situation is to increase the value of the transaction; first for your customer and second for yourself or your company. In order to do that you have to offer a *relevant* cross-sale item. If you are a grocery retailer, it makes sense to cross promote and sell products that comprise a complete meal such as pasta sauce with pasta. This pairing makes sense and is referred to as a "symmetrical complementary product." In the pasta/pasta sauce example, these two products can be shown to improve the overall purchase by improving the overall purchase. Pasta just tastes better with sauce! In order to make cross-selling work for you you'll need to try to look for product or service pairings that are complementary.

One of the decision points you'll have to make in the cross-sell situation is to decide which product or service is the lead. This can be decided by who the stronger driving partner is and letting that person/company take the lead. This can be a bit tricky as it is natural for someone to believe that their product is more desirable to the customer. Another method that can help to avoid partner conflict is the view conversion rate.

If you are able to get ahold of conversion data, this is an obvious and powerful metric to use. The conversion rate identifies the percentage of people who, when buying the "lead" product or service, choose to also buy the "promoted" product or service. If you do not have this type of metric to use as a tool the other good place to go is to your customer avatar (sales tip #28). A complete avatar (ideal customer profile) should have a list of the types of products/services that your customer consumes or needs. You can use this data in a "directional" manner to make inferences about consumption propensity.

In summary, if you want to bring real value to your prospect you'll find offers that provide a bigger value. If you can partner with other divisions in your company, do so. If that opportunity doesn't exist look for synergistic partnerships with third party companies that add value to the complete package. Your prospect will appreciate you doing this work and providing this service for them. You'll have to network to find the right partners (see #15). Remember that the sum of the parts is greater than the whole. Think value for your prospect or client!

# Training Tip: #24:
# Create Educational Seminars

Creating seminars for your clients and prospects is a tremendous way to build your brand (see training tip #1), your sales funnel (training tip #6), and a great way to network (training tip #15). Online seminars are a good way to do all of these things. But live in-person seminars are even better. The real power of this strategy is that it brings people together to network and learn how you can help them with what you have to offer.

Seminars allow you to demonstrate your competence and expertise. They provide you with an opportunity to show your prospects why they need your product or service in a personal setting. The ability to be standing in front of them in person provides flexibility to tailor the information to meet their specific needs. If you can't see them, you can't take advantage of this powerful ability to communicate in a live, interactive, and visual manner.

The great thing about seminars compared to other techniques like cold calling, advertising or other marketing outreach programs is that doing a seminar is the fastest route to going through the sales cycle. There are several key reasons why:

1. **You Are the Expert:** There's something about being in front of a group with all eyes focused on you. People automatically think that you have a message to communicate that is valuable. You will be perceived as the authority.
2. **The Audience Is Attentive:** At least in the beginning, the audience is going to listen to you. They've made a conscious decision to attend your event so they are going to be actively engaged in listening and learning from the start. This makes for the perfect selling situation. It's "almost" better than having them captive on the golf course for 4–5 hours! Your only

competition will be their cell phone, which you can respectfully ask them to turn off or silence at the beginning of the event.
3. **Fast Path to Trust:** The buy/sell relationship is all about building trust. The statistics show that it takes 6–8 quality contacts, on average, before someone is ready to buy from you. Trust is a huge factor in this process. No one will buy from you if they don't trust you. Having the ability for your audience to get to know you as an authority from the first stage helps to establish that trust factor faster than any other method available. A key element in this process is to make sure that you let your personality shine through during your presentation. Sharing personal stories about experiences that you have had with clients is a good method of doing this. They key is to connect at a personal level and the quality of your presentation and storytelling is extremely important.
4. **Show and Tell:** Another value of a seminar is the ability to show prospects the product or service you have and why it is something they should care about. You control the message. But since you control that message it is your responsibility to use that power wisely. Make sure that you are delivering real value in your presentation. The goal is to sell "yourself" first. Then you sell your product. Think about the value of the information you can impart in the event that your prospect does not become a client immediately. They should leave your seminar wiser than when they walked in.
5. **There Is Power in Groups:** If you know how to use the influence of groups, your chances of making a sale increase exponentially. Group interaction and emotion, especially if they are favorably disposed to what you have to offer, provides social proof that you've got something that people want. You don't get this in a 1:1 setting.

# Training Tip #25: Know Your "Why"

Knowing your "why" may not seem like a sales tip or strategy but it is at the core of everything you do. Why do you do what you do? What drives you in the morning to dive right into building your business? Having a vision and knowing where you are going is absolutely necessary in order to maximize your success in life.

When you know your purpose, your "why", you can focus like a laser. In fact, that is a pretty good analogy to describe the power of knowing your "why". Laser is an acronym for light amplification by stimulated emission of radiation. The interesting thing about a laser is that it only uses one wavelength of light. The visible light that we see is comprised of many wavelengths. The laser only works when one of those wavelengths is identified and then focused in a tight beam. It is so powerful that a laser can be aimed at the moon, bounced off a mirror, and returned to the earth.

Your "why" works the same way. Your "why" is a clearly defined sense of purpose that you can use to focus on attaining your goals. A clear sense of purpose enables you to focus your efforts on what matters most. Frederick Nietzsche once said, "He who has a why can endure anything." People with a passionate clear sense of purpose will do anything to achieve their objectives regardless of the odds or obstacles.

Leadership expert John Maxwell tells a story about three bricklayers. In the story, a man comes across three bricklayers who are busy at work. He asks the first bricklayer what he is doing. "I'm laying bricks," says the worker. He asks the second bricklayer the same question. "I'm putting up a wall," he said. He asks the third bricklayer the same question. "I'm building a cathedral," says the third guy. Each man had the same job, but each man's purpose was different. Their "why" is what drives them to do their job.

So how do you develop a purpose? Here's the truth of this. No one can tell you what your purpose is. You have to decide that for yourself.

You have to look deep inside yourself to determine your "why". One exercise to help you better understand yourself is to answer a series of questions. Use the following four questions to help better understand what is important to you.

1. What do you do?
2. What are you most passionate about?
3. What are your innate strengths?
4. Where do you add the greatest value?

Once you have written out the answers to these questions you are ready to draft your "why" statement. This is something that you can take your time with. Realize that once you have a statement it probably won't be the same statement your entire life. Expect that it will change as you go through life. Feel free to go back to the four questions and go through the exercise again.

There are some simple guidelines for creating your "why" statement. Your "why" should be simple and clear. It should be actionable. It should be focused on how your passion and skills can contribute to others. And, finally, it should use language that is personal and meaningful to you.

An easy sentence format you can use is as follows:

**TO _____ SO THAT _____.**

Example: "To empower individuals to discover their inner talents so that they can create a life that is filled with realized potential."

Using the above questions and format, create several "why" statements and chose that which best fits your true passions.

# Training Tip #26: Follow up like a Champion

Besides the impulse buy that you might make at the checkout line, most sales typically take place over a period of time. There is a series of steps, a process that you lead your prospect through. There is an old saying; "The fortune is in the follow-up." And prompt follow-up after the first, second, third, and every meeting is critical.

You can get all the best qualified leads in the world but they are worthless if you do not follow up. Research has found that only 10% of sales professionals follow up on a lead more than three times. Close to half of all salespeople never follow up on a lead at all!

Why is follow-up so important? Besides being the professional and courteous thing to do, research shows that 10% of sales are closed on the fourth contact. The majority of sales (80%) are made on the fifth to twelfth contact. With those statistics it's easy to see why they say, "The fortune is in the follow-up."

What constitutes good follow-up? Well, the thing that is not included in good follow-up is emailing "just to check-in". This does little to move the sale forward because you are not actively engaging the prospect in the process. Proper follow-up begins before the first meeting is even over. There should ALWAYS be an agreed upon next step. If you don't have this piece your probability of closing the deal falls precipitously.

Always do a check to see where your prospect is in the process. Do they need additional information? Do they need to confer with other people in the company before making a purchase decision? And one of the most important questions is do they have the money in this year's budget to make the purchase? Once you have these answers you can follow up appropriately.

Following up is more art than science. Like anything in life, practice makes better. The more you follow up the better you will get at it. There is no skill that you can learn or tactic you can employ that can replace building strong follow-up habits. Following up helps your prospect to remember the information that you presented. The amount of information that people forget is alarming. Studies show that within one hour people will have forgotten an average of 50 percent of the information you presented. Within the first day following your meeting they have forgotten an average of 70% of the information. Within a week, forgetting claims an average of 90% of it.

When is the right time to take a prospect off of your follow-up list? The answer is NEVER take them off your follow-up list. Sometimes prospects are just testing the waters or trying to get educated on a good or service. It may not be the right time for them to buy. The truth is you never know when the time will be right for them to need what you are selling until they actually make the purchase. The IronMan Sales Professional never takes a prospect off the list until they get an order, even if the order is, "Never call me again!"

Following up with a prospect demonstrates that you are committed to building relationships with your customers. Sales are made when you and the prospect have developed a relationship of trust. Your prospect will appreciate your professionalism, and if you orchestrate your follow-up correctly, you have shown that you care about the prospect and their business.

Lastly, the follow-up rule is not just for prospects only. You want to treat your customers with the same care and respect. Your current customers are MORE valuable than the ones to come because the cost to acquire a new customer is 7 times the cost of retaining a current one. Proper follow-up takes some work, but, in the long-run, taking these steps is critical to your success and it will pay off handsomely. The fortune really is in the follow-up!

# Training Tip #27: Put on Your Yin & Yang

All of the sales skills in the world won't help you perform at your best if your life is out of balance. What is balance in life? You often hear people talk about being out of balance in life or complaining about their life being lopsided. Usually, these complaints involve their work life and the fact that it can sometimes seem to consume all of their waking periods. For most people, work is a crucial part of their life. It pays the bills, and it gives one a sense of purpose.

Work is important, but if it seems like that is all that you do, your life is probably out of balance. This typically leads to stress, and stressed-out people are not top performing sales professionals. Living a balanced life doesn't mean you take more time from your work life by attempting to reallocate it to other parts of your life. In fact, in many cultures, this would not be possible. True balance is about what you do with the time you have.

Living a balanced life is not necessarily about time portioned between life segments. It is more about how you spend the time that you have. It is really a philosophy about the things that are important to you. A well-balanced life contains four segments:

1. **Emotional** – this includes your relationships with your friends, family, and others
2. **Mental** – this is what you think about yourself and your outlook on life
3. **Physical** – this relates to your physical health and your philosophy about exercise
4. **Spiritual** – this relates to your belief system (faith, values, etc.).

Each of these segments is important. If you give your work an inordinate amount of focus, it is likely that some or all of these areas will be lacking. That is not balance! It is important to note that this is not an issue of time. It is about focusing your attention fully on the four life areas when you are working within them.

Balance is important because there is a very high correlation between balance in life and self-reported happiness. Studies in this area show that individuals who have very high weekly working hours report an increased incidence of depression (27%), anxiety (34%), and irritability (58%). More than 40% of employees who were surveyed reported that they were neglecting other aspects of their lives because of their work.

How do you achieve balance? Achieving balance in one's life is going to be different for every individual. It will be based on their respective weighting of importance in each of the four segments of life. In other words, a formula will not meet the needs of all people. Developing a philosophy about life and your individual circumstances will provide the most fruitful results in achieving balance.

A good strategy is to follow the middle path. The middle path is not about going straight down the middle. It is not about portioning equal amounts of time to each area of your life. It's about taking each of those four segments of your life seriously and not letting any piece suffer from lack of focus.

Your life will take many turns. You may find that you are neglecting one area of your life because events in another area of your life have become time-consuming. Having the focus to be mindful of this and return attention to the neglected areas when you are able is crucial to the achievement of life balance. In many ways, your life is like a ship on the ocean. You can decide what your course will be, but the tides, the currents or a storm may push your ship off course.

A good ship's captain will deal with this by constantly adjusting the ship's navigation as necessary. You must do the same. Life is not a straight line moving from one place to another but instead a zigzag path. If you make the necessary adjustments at the right times, you'll end up at your desired destination and find balance along the way.

# Training Tip #28: Create an Avatar

Even though your product may serve a broad base of customer types, you always want to specialize. The best way to do this is to create a customer avatar (not to be confused with the James Cameron movie with the same name). An avatar can help you to understand who your ideal customer is and how to best target that person. Just because you are going to target a specific customer to sell to doesn't mean that you will limit yourself in regards to the customers that want and need your product. But it's important to note that not every customer is going to be of benefit to you.

Also, you'll want to make sure that whatever marketing dollars you have are being used to effectively reach your ideal customer. In addition, having an ideal avatar can help to focus your prospecting efforts. If you really do have several different customer types, you could even create multiple customer profiles to target if you wish.

Creating your ideal customer avatar is a fairly simple process. Here are the steps you will take to do so.

1. **Create a name for your avatar:** An avatar is not just a bunch of statistics. It is a real person. Creating a name and even a face for your avatar will help you to market to the ideal customer.
2. **List out their demographics:** Try to think about all of the attributes that your ideal customer has and write them down. Some of the attributes that you might start with are: age, gender, marital status, household income, occupation, education level, children, interests, hobbies, goals, dreams, fears or frustrations. These demographics will be used to design the product/services you are creating to serve your ideal customer.
3. **Write a story:** Create a story about your ideal customer. Make this story about why they like your product or service. Be as descriptive and creative as you can. You may find in your story

that you've developed ways that you can reach them or the message you want to create to help solve their problem.
4. **Research your avatar:** Now that you've created your ideal avatar it's time to do some research. Remember your avatar is a real person. You'll need to find them in real life to learn more about them. Facebook and LinkedIn are two great places to start. Another place is to look for local meetups where there are people who match your avatar. Once you've found them you should reach out to them to get to know them better. Ask for their permission to interview them. Now's your opportunity to ask deep, probing questions that will allow you to flesh out your avatar more.

If you have more than one ideal customer, create additional avatars and repeat the steps above. You'll also want to revisit your avatar from time to time to see if the profile you created is still relevant. Over time and as you get to know more about your ideal customer, your avatar may evolve. Don't be afraid to make some changes to it. The use of a customer avatar is a very well-practiced technique in marketing. A lesser-used technique is the use of "negative avatars".

Creating a negative avatar can be as useful as creating your ideal customer avatar. What is a negative avatar? A negative avatar is exactly as it sounds. It is a representation of the person that you do not want as a customer. You should go through the same three steps listed above. You can forget step number four. It probably wouldn't be much fun anyway! The key here is to focus on the personal characteristics of why the negative avatar is someone you won't want to work with. You can use this avatar to confirm and reaffirm your decision about not working with them when the question arises.

# Training Tip #29: Follow a Process

*"If you can't describe what you are doing as a process, you don't know what you are doing." ~ W. Edwards Deming*

What is a process? According to Webster's Dictionary, it is defined as "a series of actions or operations conducing to an end a particular end." The "end" we're interested in is the sale! Process is the key to riches. If you have a CRM system (see training tip #8) you are using some type of process called a sales funnel. This is an important process! What lies underneath the sales funnel are detailed steps used to get a prospect in the funnel and move them through it to a decision to buy or not to buy. That would include using call scripts, FAQ's, objection answers, presentations, proposal templates, and all of the activities that are internal and external to your company to closing the sale.

Whether you are aware of it or not, process is in everything we do. If you brush your teeth (and I hope you do), you follow a process. Here is an example of that process. There are a *series of steps that you perform in order* to brush your teeth.

1. You take out your toothbrush
2. You run it under the faucet to dampen it
3. You apply the toothpaste
4. You brush your teeth
5. You rinse your toothbrush under water again to clean it
6. You store it away for future use

What happens if you skip a step like applying the toothpaste? Probably nothing at first, but if you keep doing it then it won't be as effective—and you might end up getting cavities, which is exactly the opposite of the goal for brushing your teeth in the first place.

The principles of process also hold true with cooking. If you don't follow a recipe or exclude a crucial ingredient, you risk making something that tastes really bad! The sales process is no different. If you have designed a solid process and you don't use it, you risk not being as successful as you could be. In fact, if you skip a step or perform the steps in the wrong order, be prepared to be outsold by the salesperson whose execution of the process is on the mark.

There are basically four types of sales processes; 1) the dynamic sales process, 2) the formal sales process, 3) the informal sales process, and 4) the random sales process. Which is the best process to employ? Well, you can probably use your intuition to guess that the random process is the least effective.

A random process is exactly as it sounds. In this process, each sales professional is allowed to use their own method for selling. And, like anything in life, you'll always have the few at the top that have figured it out and the rest are underperformers. In fact, studies in technology sales using this type of process show success rates at only 40%.

The second from the best method is the formal sales process. It uses a fixed set of sales processes that everyone must comply with. Success rates in the same industry increase to almost 46%. But the biggest sales success rates achieved are by those who use the dynamic sales process. This process uses a defined selling model that is actively modified for the changing competitive landscape. You follow a set of steps but as situations arise that warrant changes to the process, you make the modification and move forward. The success rate for those who use the dynamic selling model increases to 55%.

You may think that 55% may not seem like a very high number. But it is certainly better than "chance". That percentage DOES NOT factor in the soft selling skills of the sales professional; a professional with average soft sales skills who follows a process should be able to close a sale more than half of the time. In other words, following a process has a huge influence on your ability to close the deal.

# Training Tip #30: Do the Difficult Things First

Brian Tracy calls doing the difficult things first "eating the frog." If you want to start your day off right, you'll do it by completing the most difficult task first. You'll be more energized (or relieved) when you get that task done and you can use that power and sense of accomplishment to carry you through the day.

There are some pretty strong reasons for doing the tough stuff first. It's probably not surprising that there is a lot of psychology in successful task attainment. People don't like to do things that are uncomfortable, no matter how beneficial that activity might be once it is completed. So, one goal for dealing with this would be to attempt to make the difficult task more enjoyable.

Behavioral researchers have discovered that one of the most effective ways to create an enjoyable experience in task completion is to pack in the painful parts of the experience early in the process. It's kind of like ripping the band-aid off instead of peeling it off slowly. It hurts more, but the pain is over quicker. Psychologically, people prefer experiences that get better over time; they are less tolerant of painful experiences that are drawn out. So it's better to get to the hard stuff first and get it out of the way.

The other reason that you want to dive right into the hard stuff first is because procrastination is a productivity killer. You need to understand that the reason people procrastinate is a completely natural mechanism of protection. Your subconscious mind will work to protect you from things that are uncomfortable or painful. You may not even be consciously aware that you put things off because your mind does this automatically. People often choose to work on "filler" tasks because they are quick, easy to accomplish, and provide instant gratification when they are complete. This instant gratification is from a dopamine rush you're getting. And that powerful reward makes you keep doing the thing that makes you unproductive.

The problem is that most people don't recognize when to stop working on filler tasks. They feel good so you keep doing them. And the longer the tough tasks stay on your plate the harder it will become to do the thing you're dreading. Choosing to front-load pain and discomfort isn't just a choice that applies to daily tasks and errands, it can also be used to nudge you toward the goals you have that you tend to procrastinate on.

Here's how to get started. Think about the anticipation of the start of a race for a triathlete. Imagine it's you and you're at the starting line. The first event in the triathlon is the swim. Imagine that the water is cold, it's rough, and you have at least an hour of non-stop swimming in front of you. Along the way there will be people pushing, shoving, elbowing you, and kicking you in the face. How do you start?

There is a very simple yet powerful method, perfected by Mel Robbins in her book *The 5 Second Rule* (not to be confused with the rule of the same name regarding dropped food on the floor). The 5 Second Rule is a form of metacognition, which is an awareness and understanding of your own thought processes. Consciously understanding that procrastination is part of your brain's natural operation and then taking action to interrupt that natural operation for your betterment is how the technique works. Using the technique will allow you to interrupt your procrastination behavior and engage the prefrontal cortex to get you moving in the right direction. It's a simple countdown method. It goes like this: "Ready … set … 5, 4, 3 2, 1, Go!" Just dive in and start swimming. Start your most difficult task of the day the same way. **Ready … set … 5, 4, 3 2, 1, Go!**

# Training Tip #31: Do the Easy Things Last

This training tip is a continuation from tip #30. It's sort of the yin and yang of tasks. You've got to balance the tough tasks with the easy tasks. In tip #30, the premise of doing the hard things first was to make sure you were able to achieve the most out of your day by completing the most valuable tasks and not letting procrastination get in the way. All that said, there is only one instance where doing an easy thing first can be valuable—to create momentum and emotion. This is often referred to as "constructive procrastination".

One of the most difficult parts of tackling your daily task list is just getting started. Using the countdown method described in training tip #30 is one way to do this. Constructive procrastination is another method you can use. Constructive procrastination makes this an easier process because working on easy tasks requires a smaller mental commitment than if you tackled difficult tasks first.

It doesn't matter how gung ho you are about starting your day, everyone has that point where getting going is a challenge. And if this happens to you, it can be a deterrent to your productivity. In this instance, it makes a lot of sense to save the difficult tasks for when you're in more of a groove. Do something small first, get into the groove, then immediately get going with the big stuff.

In the 2014 University of Texas Commencement Address, Admiral William H. McRaven talks about the importance of making your bed in the morning. Posted on YouTube, it has gotten millions of views. Doing this simple task gives you momentum. It chalks one task off the list and no matter how the day goes, you'll come home to a neatly made bed that you can comfortably crawl into at night.

If making your bed in the morning isn't your thing, pick some other easy and quick task to start your day. Just make sure it doesn't detract from doing the tougher, more valuable and more rewarding things you added to your list from training tip #30. You'll gain momentum and feel good about it.

If you are doing the harder, more productive tasks first you're well on your way to making the most productive day you can. But when do you begin the easier tasks? Research shows that workers showed that 2:55 PM is the least productive time of day. As fatigue of a hard-worked morning sets in you begin to become less motivated and active. The afternoon is a good time to log research about your prospects and plan next steps. It's also a good time to preplan your next day's activities (training tip #32).

The best way to end the day is to have some accomplishments. The more you have the better you feel. Always try to end your day by accomplishing something small. It doesn't matter if the accomplishment was big or small. You still get that same dopamine rush regardless of the scope of the task. And smaller tasks are easier to accomplish!

The afternoon is the perfect time to do the things that don't take a high level of cognitive effort but are still important. You still want to be productive but late afternoon is the time to begin to plan your wind-down. How you end your day is as important as how you begin it. Your afternoon is a lead in to the evening.

How you go into your evening can help determine the type of sleep you get, and the quality of the sleep you get determines how you will begin your next day. Your sleep helps your brain to work properly. While you're sleeping, your brain is preparing for the next day by forming new pathways to help you learn and remember information. It is a cycle that goes from one day to the next. So, planning how you spend your day and what you do during that time is key to your productivity and happiness. Make sure to go back and review training tip #22 for more on daily planning.

# Training Tip #32: Preplan Your Day Using Lists

*"Success depends upon previous preparation, and without such preparation there is sure to be failure." ~ Confucius*

This training tip is a bit of a continuation of training tip #22. If you are planning your day, you are way ahead of the game in terms of productivity. But often the forgotten part of daily planning is the review and preplanning for the next day. By now, you know that those who are at the top of their game, peak performers, follow a daily planning process. The act of daily planning leads to greater personal productivity gains than any other strategy. Daily planning includes a "review" of the day's activities as well as preplanning by listing the top three things that you'd like to accomplish tomorrow.

Getting your day planned tightly is crucial to every project you plan to complete, long or short term. Daily tasks are important because they lead to weekly accomplishments and then monthly accomplishments. How much you accomplish really gets down to refining how you plan your day. But planning your day alone isn't enough. You also need to employ certain techniques to ensure that you actually see your plan through and meet your goals.

There are many methods and commercial programs available for becoming more productive and managing daily tasks. Unfortunately, the current success rate for effective daily planning is very low. So why do most people fail at planning? The simple truth is that they fail because they do not take a focused approach to daily task organization. When you are planning to complete big projects, you first need to focus on the most important components. Once you have identified those components, you need to focus on the daily activities that will help you to complete them.

The best approach to achieving focused daily planning is to "pre-plan" how you want your tomorrow to go. The most effective way to do this is with the use of "task lists". You can begin by spending the last 15 minutes of your work day making your list for tomorrow's work day. Start by constructing a solid foundation for your daily tasks and then get into the details. This foundation is extremely important but fairly simple to build. The first step is to build a master list of activities or a master task list. A master task list is a list of your most productive and most important activities.

Productive activities are those things you do that will give you the greatest return for your time. Don't fall into the trap of writing down tasks or items that you would probably accomplish as part of your daily routine. Some people like to do this for the sake of getting to cross things off the list. This can be satisfying but it's not really the best use of your planning time.

Focus on writing a list that encompasses activities that will help meet larger goals but not daily tasks that are part of your everyday routine. The idea is to achieve larger end goals, not to get to the end of each day with a completed list but no effort toward your ultimate goals. Be strategic in creating your daily list. Peak performers are able to discriminate between daily chores and goal-oriented activities. Learn to be picky!

Your master list will contain your annual goals as well as other important tasks that you identify from day to day. You will use your master list to feed the creation of your daily list. When you are building your daily task list, refer to the master list of items. Carefully choose those items that you feel you can accomplish during the time you have each day. List creation is part of the pre-planning process. Don't skip it because it's the foundation and is as important as how you plan at the beginning of your day.

# Training Tip #33: Plan Your Sales Calls

Preplanning your sales calls is just as important as planning your day (sales tip #22). The success of your sales calls largely depends on the time and preplanning that you put into them. As a practice, you should plan every customer/prospect encounter in detail. You should write a plan for the call including everything from your goals to your expected next steps, and a call to action for the prospect. It is easiest to preplan if you follow a set of recommended guidelines. Listed below are a series of steps, which, if followed, will create more successful opportunities and stronger customer relationships.

**Step 1 - Research the company:** Why would you ever purposely walk into a call with no knowledge of the company? It's a waste of everyone's time, including your own. Do a search on the company's history. What are their products? Who are their customers? What is their status in the marketplace? Is their company shrinking, growing or stagnant? Who are its competitors? You should know the answers to these questions and many more prior to your call.

**Step 2 - Research your contact:** Getting to know your contact is just as important as the company they work for. This can be just as easy as the company research. Start with a simple online search of the person. Use Google and the most popular social media accounts. The number one social media platform for business is LinkedIn. If your contact has a profile, you'll be able to learn a lot about their experience as well as possibly gain insight to reasons why they may buy.

Another good reason to research your contact's background is that knowledge can help to create opportunities for conversation. Remember one of the most important paths to building a trusted relationship is finding common ground. Everyone has something in common. Knowing your contact's history can help you to find that common ground.

**Step 3 - Do a competitive analysis:** You should know who the company's biggest competitors are. How do they differentiate themselves (unique selling proposition)? What types of selling strategy or marketing do they do? What image are they trying to portray? When you know these things, you can have an intelligent conversation with your prospect or customer contact about their business. Showing you are knowledgeable about the issues that they face helps to build trust.

**Step 4 - Establish your goals:** The end goal is always to make a sale. But that may not be the specific goal for this call. Remember that sales is a process. Usually, you can't skip over crucial steps to get there. Sometimes that happens and when it does it's pretty nice! But that is not the norm.

Have a goal for the call that moves you through the sales cycle. It could be to get to the next meeting, to set up a demonstration of the product or to gather information needed to prepare a quotation. It doesn't matter what the goal is as long as it continues to move you through the cycle.

**Step 5 - Plan call questions:** No matter how much pre-call research you do there will always be bit of information that you won't be able to find. As in many interactions, the quality of your call can depend on the quality of your questions. Not only should you have a list of questions pre-prepared but you should also be prepared to interactively ask questions during the call. The right questions don't just uncover the data you need, they also show your prospect how much you care about understanding his or her needs.

**Step 6 - Prepare yourself mentally:** Always prepare yourself mentally prior to a call. You've already done the background research and preparation but you can't forget your personal presentation. You'll need to get into a positive mental state. Take a breath, visualize how you want the meeting to go. Your emotional state will come out in your presentation, good or bad.

# Training Tip #34: Watch What You Eat

Watch what you eat and drink, how much you sleep, and how much you exercise. Often overlooked (until we look in the mirror and see 20 extra pounds) is the attainment of a well-balanced life through optimal health. Proper nutrition, exercise, and rest are of paramount importance to becoming a top sales performer. Health and exercise are often overlooked because they take discipline, hard work, and usually it's not something that you want to do. It usually takes a second seat to work, family, and everything else. But you must make time to care for your body!

Why is this a training tip? There are several key reasons why health is an important factor to becoming a top sales professional. First, you can't operate at your top capability if you are dealing with debilitating health issues. You won't have the physical energy or mental acumen to face challenges without proper health. Secondly, once you have attained sales success, you will need all your physical and mental skills just to maintain your status. Lastly, you want to be able to enjoy the many benefits that come with being a top sales professional and maintaining your health ensures that you live long enough to do so!

Maybe you want to retire early and enjoy life, but if you don't take care of your health, you won't be able to enjoy the fruits of your labors. Even if you do live long, you might be plagued with health issues that will surely detract from fully enjoying life. You could end up spending all the income you earned as a top performing sales professional on medical bills.

Eating "clean" is a key dietary factor and is more directly effective than physical exercise on your overall health. The ideal situation would be to eliminate all junk food and other unhealthy snacks from your diet. The reality is this is probably an unrealistic goal for most people. The next best course of action is to eat the most nutritious meals possible and to keep junk food to a minimum. The real key here is moderation. Learn to moderate not only the consumption of foods that aren't optimal for your health but also the quantity of food you consume overall.

Part of a proper diet is ensuring that you get proper daily hydration. Most people are mildly dehydrated and don't even know it. If you are thirsty, you are already dehydrated. Make it a habit of sipping water throughout the day. Something as simple as proper water intake can have a significant impact on your cognitive abilities. Water makes up approximately 75% of the brain. It is an essential element in ensuring proper neurological transmissions.

Another key to good health is adequate exercise. You don't need to train like a marathoner to be healthy, for like all other aspects of becoming a peak performing sales professional, it's about moderate and steady progress, not short spurts of energy. Start by getting out of your chair and moving your body every day.

One of the most common excuses people give is that they don't have the time to exercise. This is a very poor excuse. It doesn't matter what your current physical condition is or even if you have some type of physical impairment. There is always something that can be done to stretch your muscles, get your heart pumping, and increase your breathing efficiency.

Top sales performers always find the time to exercise. The absolute minimum you should strive for is thirty minutes of moderate exercise each day. Discipline yourself to get up one hour earlier in order to achieve some type of daily exercise. If you just can't get out of bed any earlier, figure out what you're going to give up in order to create space for exercise in the rest of your day. A great disposable pastime is television. If you find you can't give up your news hour, put a treadmill in front of your television and exercise while you get your news all in the same hour. The road to success is paved with courage and discipline. Having great physical health will help you become a top sales performer and it will help you stay that way.

# Training Tip #35: Listen

One of the areas that many people could get better at is listening. If you are a sales professional, you don't have a choice but to be a <u>really good</u> listener. You've heard the old saying; "You have two ears and one mouth and you should use them all equally." That's a pretty good start to being a good listener. But there is so much more to it than just using your body parts equally. You need to be an active listener.

The University of Colorado defines active listening as: "A way of listening and responding to another person that improves mutual understanding." There are actually three levels of listening you can utilize in active listening.

**Level 1:** At this level you are listening to your inner voice. Most people operate at this level. This is a passive listening mode and is what comes naturally to all people. In order to move to higher levels of listening, you'll have to do some skill building. Usually when you are listening to people speak at this level, your mind is actively thinking about how you will respond or what you will say next.

**Level 2:** At this level you are intently listening to another person. This level of listening take a conscious effort. It's a skill that must be developed. At this listening level, you are actively paying attention to what the other person is saying. Unlike level 1 listening you are not thinking about what you want to say to respond to the other person. Your full attention is on the person you are listening to.

**Level 3:** At this level, you are listening to others in the context of their entire surroundings. Sometimes this is called global listening. This is the highest level of listening. At this level of listening you are paying close attention to the words of the person that you are listening to and also the meanings and feelings behind these words. This is important because not everyone says what they really mean. Sometimes you have to "read between the lines".

Knowing the three levels of listening is not enough. You will actually have to practice in order to gain proficiency. Here are some things you can do to improve your listening skills.

One of the first things you can do is be present. Nothing is ruder than answering your phone or reading texts while you are with another person. Unless you are an on-call medical professional or in some other profession where you are legitimately are on call there's no need to be watching your phone. Make sure that any other distractions are eliminated. If you are sitting across from someone in a public place, your eyes should be on the person across from you, not darting around the room at everything else that moves. Keep eye contact with them.

Actively listening means that you do not interrupt the other person when they are speaking. People will respect you when you respect what they have to say. Hear what they have to say, pause (a five count is good), and then respond. This pause implies that you are taking seriously what they have to say.

Another technique you can use is to ask open-ended questions. This allows the person you are speaking with to play a greater role in the conversation. Because they are talking more you'll have to listen more! When it's time for you to speak, paraphrase what the other person said to be sure you understood them correctly.

Active listening also entails watching the other person's body language. Remember that only 7% of communication is conveyed by the words you use. Fifty-five percent of communication is translated non-verbally, and 38% is indicated by the tone and inflection of the voice.

Using active listening helps you to fully understand what the prospect has communicated to you and it demonstrates respect for your prospect, giving you a leg-up in the sales process.

# Training Tip #36: Practice, Practice, Practice

Don't ever do a sales presentation cold. Sales professionals don't "wing it" or even do a presentation "off the cuff". An effective sales presentation goes beyond just reading the PowerPoint slides (BTW – don't do this ... it's insulting). Rarely is there anyone in life who is a "natural". Everyone who is an expert at their craft has practiced a lot!

If you've ever played golf, you know that there are so many parts of the game that take different kinds of practice for it all to come together. Even if you naturally have a good golf swing, you'll never be a good or even great golfer, unless you practice. Talent is never enough in life to be a success.

When someone looks as natural as Tiger Woods with a golf club it is typical for people to think that they achieved success because they were really talented. That is a false belief! Greatness in any field is something that takes years of hard work, attention to detail, and determination. Being the best at what you do as a sales professional is no different. It will take lots of practice.

Sadly, the majority of salespeople "wing it". That's why most never achieve super success in their careers. If you've been around for any period of time in business you've seen these people, it's usually a train wreck. The typical salesperson receives an average of three days of sales training in their entire career! And practice? Forget about it! Since you are reading this book this is probably not you!

There are many forms of practice and you should use as many of them as you can. Go ahead and incorporate some of these into your sales training regimen.

**The Shower:** If you practice in the shower you'll have the content of what you want to present memorized. Why? Because you can't take notes in the shower! You many not say the same thing every time you practice, but you'll certainly remember the key points of what you want to communicate.

**The Video Presentation:** Video tape yourself and watch it over and over again. What you'll mostly be concerned about is your body language. Are you using your body effectively to communicate your message? Remember that more than 50% of communication is non-verbal.

**The Mirror:** One of the best places to practice your sales presentation is in front of the mirror. You'll can watch yourself in real time and make corrections and adjustments on the fly.

**The Friend:** Some people think it is harder to present in front of friends, family or peers. Other people think that it is a non-threatening audience and it is the easiest presentation. Either way, you should do it! If it's hard in front of friends the real thing will be easier and if it's easy in front of friends you'll build self-confidence.

**A Trainer or Coach:** If you have access to a business coach or a sales trainer this is a great way to improve your abilities fast. They'll have the experience to quickly identify points of correction as well as your strengths so that you capitalize on them.

**Practice On-the-Job:** Practicing on the job is the <u>last place</u> you should practice! Never make this the first practice spot. You should have many hours of practice before you ever get to this part. You will still do a "post meeting analysis" of your presentation. Pat yourself on the back for the parts that you did well and identify the portions of your performance where you will improve.

**A Simple Formula:** The rule for speaking professionals is to practice 1 hour for each minute of your presentation. That's right! Thirty minutes equals 30 hours of practice.

# Training Tip #37: Put Out Positive Energy

Make sure you are only communicating in a positive state. It doesn't matter if you are making phone calls and your prospect/client won't see you. They can "hear" your emotions in your voice.

A sales professional without passion and energy is just like a car that has the wrong type of fuel in it. It doesn't run smoothly, it knocks and doesn't start easily and you don't know if it will make it to your destination. Your attitude is the fuel that you put into your profession.

Being able to monitor and control your attitude will have the greatest impact on your work performance, your relationships and almost everyone around you. One of the greatest powers that we all have is the ability to choose an inner dialogue of self-encouragement and self-motivation. Alternatively, we can choose one of self-defeat and self-pity. It's as simple as that.

There are a plethora of occurrences in today's world that can cause you to lose your passion and energy. It could be a negative work situation, financial problems, relationship problems or even illnesses. All of us encounter difficult times, disappointments, successes, and failures. The key is to realize it's not what happens to you that matters; it's how you choose to respond. Do you respond with negativity or do you treat the tough lessons, the hurdles in the road, as part of the road?

It is very important to learn to manage your emotional state daily and recharge your passion for your business or for your life. Only in a state of recharge can you perform at higher levels and give your customers or prospects the ultimate experience.

Emotion is energy. Always remember that people feel the energy that you put out and will mirror that emotional state. Positive energy will bring you positive results. Negative energy will give you negative results. It's simple science.

Here are a couple of tips to help you maintain a positive emotional state.

- **Increase your levels of physical activity level.** You can't have an IronMan Mindset without involving the physical! Physical activity of any kind—a walk, a gym workout or playing a sport—will revitalize and regenerate your body and mind. As little as 30 minutes a day can make a huge difference in the way you feel physically and emotionally. A simple smile can also be a powerful tool. Hold a smile for at least 20 seconds. Smiling lowers your heart rate and reduces that anxious response you feel, even when your smile is forced.
- **Appreciate the good.** There's plenty of it around you if you stop, listen, look and notice it. A great tool you can use in the morning, evening or whenever you need it is to write down three things you are thankful for. You'll be amazed at how quickly your mood will shift from a negative state to a positive one.
- **Use positive affirmations.** Use affirmations to start your day or to help fortify you when things are tough. Affirmations are valuable tools, used to move our reality in positive directions. It doesn't matter what your experiences have been in regards to family, culture or environment or even how old you are. Anyone can benefit from the effective use of positive affirmations. Use positive, self-directed affirmations to create the self-fulfilling prophecies that you desire for your life.

A positive attitude can go a long way in forging long-lasting customer relationships. Monitor, regulate, and watch your sales grow!

# Training Tip #38: Use the Phone

Cold calling is dead if you believe the ads all over the internet. Suffice to say that cold calling isn't what is used to be. Prospects aren't waiting by the phone for your call, hoping you have the solution to their problems.

Quite the opposite is the case. It may not be a favorite prospecting method, and it's certainly not the sexiest, but it is still being employed by many companies worldwide. It's alive, even if it isn't what it used to be. Believe it or not, cold calling is actually one of the most targeted, efficient and effective ways to reach potential customers. Nothing beats having a real conversation with a prospect. You can achieve much higher levels of communication and understanding than with a simple email. There are five (5) basic areas to focus on to make the most of cold calling.

1. **Set Your Goal:** The first thing you need to do is determine your goal. Too many new salespeople, and even non-salespersons, think that the goal of cold calling is to make a sale. It's not! Think about it honestly, how willing are you to make a purchase from someone you don't know on the first phone call? Usually, you can't wait to get off the phone and get back to your day! The primary goal of cold calling should be to earn another exposure to the prospect. It may be another phone call, a promise to do something then talk at another time or maybe even a face-to-face meeting.

2. **Use a Script:** It is important to create a script. Every good salesperson creates a script to use in their cold calling. It doesn't matter how well you know the product or how experienced you are at selling it, the script will help to ensure that you communicate the main points and that you do it in a timely fashion. It also helps to keep you focused. Remember that your goal is to create the opportunity to get another exposure. You don't want the prospect to control the conversation and potentially lose the chance to ever talk to them again!

3. **Practice:** Practice, practice, practice. Practice will make you better at anything in life, especially cold calling. If you are new to cold calling, this will increase your confidence. Practice is "almost" like the real thing. This gives you a great opportunity to practice your pitch as well as your responses to questions and how to defer questions until the next exposure. You can never get enough practice and you'll be much better once you do the real thing.

4. **Make the Call:** Persistence is the key here. You don't want to harass your prospects but you want to make sure that you are doing everything you can to get the first contact. One simple method you can use is the 3-2-message rule. That means that you attempt to reach the contact three times during the day; early morning, early afternoon, and late afternoon/early evening. You do this for two days in a row. If you still don't reach them it's time to leave a message and move on to the next phase of reaching your prospect. It may or it may not be through a phone call.

5. **Ask for the Next Step:** The last thing to do is to ask for the next exposure. Never leave a call without getting this. Sometimes it is only the permission to call again at a later, more convenient time. But you have to do it. Dental practices are the best at getting this done. Have you ever left a dentist office without the receptionist asking to get another appointment on the calendar? Of course not! This is called booking a meeting from a meeting or BAMFAM. If you don't do this, the prior four steps are almost wasted.

Obviously, there are lots of other things that are important in a cold call and even in these five areas there are a number of aspects that you should give greater focus. Focus on these five areas and enjoy greater cold calling success!

# Training Tip #39: Use Non-Successes to Improve

There is no such thing as failure. There are only non-successes. The only person who fails is the one who quits. A winner uses non-successes as learning experiences to improve their skills. Also, remember that <u>wisdom</u> is only gained through non-successes. There is an old saying; "Fail early, fail fast, and fail often."

One of the major reasons people fail to achieve their dreams is that they are not taught the process of goal attainment. Specifically, that failure, or "non-successes," is part of the process. Society celebrates winners. It lets losers slink off into the shadows of obscurity. But if you talk to every winner, they will tell you the same thing; the journey that led them to this point was filled with many non-successes. They understand that it is a continual process of learning until the desired result is achieved.

They understand that the three P's are at work.

### Patience + Persistence = Progress

In order to gain progress, one must be persistent, even in the face of successive non-successes. An even bigger component is patience. We live in an always "on", fast-paced, fast-service society. People expect progress instantaneously. However, that's not the way it works in the real world. Most progress of substance doesn't happen instantaneously. And, unfortunately, the majority of people don't understand the three P's and they give up after their first non-success.

What do Thomas Edison, Katy Perry, J.K. Rowling, Oprah Winfrey, Jim Carrey, Bill Gates, James Dyson, Stephen King, Colonel Sanders, and Henry Ford all have in common? At some point along their journey to fulfill the potential of their dreams, they had so many significant non-successes that most people would categorize them as abject failures.

Dyson failed 5,126 times before he succeeded in perfecting his famous vacuum cleaner. It is reported that it took Edison over 10,000 attempts before he created a stable version of the incandescent light bulb. Famous author Stephen King was rejected by over 30 publishers before he found one for his first book, *Carrie*. Jobless, divorced, penniless, and with a dependent child, Rowling was rejected by 12 major publishers before she found one to accept her *Harry Potter* novel.

**Still not convinced? How about these people?**

- Beethoven's music teacher once told him that, as a composer, he was hopeless.
- Charles Darwin's father told him he would amount to nothing and would be a disgrace to himself and his family.
- Walt Disney was fired by the editor of a newspaper because he, Disney, had "no good ideas."
- When Thomas Edison was a boy, his teacher told him he was too stupid to learn anything.
- Einstein was four years old before he spoke and his teachers told him he would never amount to much.
- Henry Ford's first two automobile businesses failed.
- Michael Jordan was cut from his high school basketball team.
- Ray Kroc failed as a real estate salesperson before coming up with the McDonald's idea.
- Isaac Newton failed at running the family farm and did poorly in school.

**Got the picture now?** The only limit you have in life is the limit you set on yourself. Non-successes are part of the process. Embrace them and use the three P's to create success.

# Training Tip #40: Read a Book

Read a book. In fact, read many books! Research shows that 85% of people who make at least $160,000 per year routinely read books on education, their career, and self-improvement (see #13). Conversely, according to the Jenkins Group, 42% of college graduates never read another book after college, 80% of US families did not buy or read a book last year, and 57% of new books are not read to completion. And this is one of the reasons why it is a small percentage of people who earn the most money. Self-development books are a low risk investment and they carry a very high reward to risk ratio.

Why read a book versus a blog, magazine or article? Actually, you should read all of those things. But books are a little different. Books give you greater depth on a subject. Books are usually a bit longer than an article. A hundred pages or more versus a few pages in an article allows you to more fully explore a particular theme or theory.

Another benefit to reading a book is that it allows you to focus more. When you read something online, you tend to skim the material. It is written in such a manner that you can read it quickly and easily. Online paragraphs tend to be only three sentences long. There are lots of subheadings. Conversely, books tend to contain more complex sentences and are devoid of lots of subheadings. The breadth and depth of the content actually forces you to focus more in order to fully intellectualize what you are reading.

Then there is the cost factor. That's right, you typically have to make an investment in order to get a book. Usually reading a blog is free. Most people tend to put greater value on things they invest in versus those things that they get for free. Because of this, there is a higher likelihood of people attempting to extract value out of the investment they make by trying to incorporate the things they learn into their lives.

A good practice or habit to form is to set aside a period of time every day to read something that is targeted to the development or growth you wish to achieve. It doesn't need to be a lot of time to start. As little as 30 minutes a day for a full year is the equivalent of taking three college classes. Besides that acquisition of knowledge, there are a number of other benefits that can be derived from this daily habit such as:

1. **You turn knowledge into wisdom:** Some say that knowledge is power. This is not true. Applied knowledge is power. Many personal growth books will have exercises that allow you to put your new-found knowledge into action in your life. This is where the real value of increased knowledge comes from.
2. **You can become or stay inspired:** When you are reading an inspiring book every day, you flood your brain with positive thoughts, ideas, and aspirations. If you understand the science behind energy, you will know that positive energy can go a long way in helping you to achieve your goals. You'll be inspired to make better choices and take positive actions.
3. **Books are always there:** You may not carry a physical book with you every day but chances are that you carry your mobile device or phone with you. In these instances, a book reading app on your device is a great way to always have a book with you.
4. **You build your dream:** Sometimes you need a little inspiration or an example of what could be possible. Books can provide stories of people who have achieved what you wish to achieve. It gives you the opportunity to shatter self-limiting beliefs and expand your perception of what you can achieve for yourself.

# Training Tip #41: Do Not Multitask

Most people wish they had more time in the day to accomplish the things they want to get done in their lives. The reality is that we all have the same twenty-four hours in a day. Some people are just better at using that time effectively than others.

One strategy that people use to deal with the issue of maximizing time is multitasking. The common belief is that you can maximize your time by working on multiple tasks at once. However, this concept of effective time usage is misleading.

In reality, multitasking is a huge time waster that *nearly everyone* is guilty of. How many times have you talked on the phone to someone and realized that you were doing something else like typing emails, checking your text or even doodling? Have you ever been caught at it? If so, you'll know how disrespectful this was to the person on the other end of the phone.

Even on a phone call, when the other party can't see you, people can hear how engaged you are in the conversation by the tone of your voice and the manner in which you respond to what they are saying. You'll need to practice active listening (see training tip #35) to stay focused on the conversation. The mind innately wanders from one topic to another. Like a small child, whose attention you can't keep, the human brain tends to operate the same way.

The advent of electronic media and transportable technology is also to blame for the rise of multitasking. Texting while driving, listening to music and working, doing multiple activities while you are talking on the phone, watching a video on a TV or iPad while you are studying are all common multitasking activities that people engage in.

 Are you guilty of it? Come on … admit it. Of course you are. Do you think you are really getting anything done? Sure you are. The real question should be are you doing all these tasks really well? Research shows that you are not! Since the 1990s, when the term multitasking was borrowed from the definition of a computer executing a series of commands at once, physiologists have studied this human phenomenon.

Many people believe that they can complete two or more tasks as effectively as they can complete one task. However, numerous studies show that people who multitask show severe interference in accomplishing even the simplest of tasks effectively. In fact, the concept of the human mind functioning to accomplish many tasks at once is a bit of a misnomer. Many researchers believe that the human mind can only fully focus on accomplishing one task at a time, and a bottleneck of activity results in loss of productivity or even the ability to successfully accomplish a task. A better descriptor of multitasking would be rapid task switching.

When a person switches from one task to another, the brain pauses and restarts according to the new information or reference point. Studies show that this pause and restart leads to slower response time and more errors in task completion. The time to switch from one task to another might waste only $1/10^{th}$ of a second. That doesn't sound like a lot, but if you do a lot of switching in a day, it can add up to a loss of 40% of your productivity.

So, what does making mistakes have to do with time management? Well, if you have to repeat a task or make corrections because of errors, how efficient is that? Did multitasking really make you more productive in this instance? It didn't! In fact, studies show that task completion time can almost double because of error correction versus tasks that are completed in a sequential manner.

If you are a multitasker, maybe you now see that this is not an attribute that will serve you well. Slow down, plan your tasks, and focus. You'll be more productive, operate in a less frenetic manner, and you'll have more time to do the things you want to accomplish in life.

# Training Tip #42: Be a Storyteller

There is an old saying in sales; "Facts tell but stories sell." The best way to communicate information to a prospect about your product is to tell a story. People tend to relate stories to their own experiences and stories are a great vehicle to stir up memories that evoke emotions. Stories capture attention, they motivate people to take action, and they help to transform their beliefs and change their minds.

A number of studies show approximately 63 percent of people remembered the facts of a story while only about 5 percent remembered the same facts when they were presented without a story. Stories come in all types of varieties; myths, legends, fairy tales, fables, ghost tales, hero stories, and epic adventures (think Homer). Stories are used to communicate all types of information.

Many psychologists believe that storytelling is one of the many things that define our humanity because they think that humans are the only animals that create and tell stories. It is a unique form of communication and stories told verbally have been passed down over the millennia.

There is a really good reason why stories are an effective means of sales communication. Besides being fun to listen to, they stimulate the emotional side of our brain. This is important because there is a large body of research that shows that the decision to "buy" is an emotional decision. People purchase on emotion first then they use their cognitive reasoning to justify their purchase decision. Engaging the left side of the brain with an emotional story helps to create fertile ground for a product or service sale.

In business, like in other parts of your life, you'll need to convey information in a manner that is conducive to the situation. There are a few types of stories that are commonly used in sales situations.

Here are a few that you can use to get started with storytelling:

- **Vision Stories:** A vision story is used to communicate your vision and inspire others to act. A common vision story is one that talks about how a product saved a company money.
- **Your Story:** You story is a personal story about who you are. Its purpose is to communicate to the listener information about you that will help them form a connection or establish your authority in a certain area.
- **The Passion Story:** This is another personal story that explains your passion. It could be why you believe in your product, why it fits with your personal mission statement (see training tip #2).
- **Your Company Story:** Besides yourself, your prospect needs to know about your company. Tell them a story that is meaningful. Why does the company exist? How is it helping people? A great place to start is the company's mission statement.

Creating your own story is important in the sales process. It doesn't matter which of the story types you choose, the constructive elements of the story are the same. There are three main components that you'll want to include.

1. **The Conflict:** What is the problem that you, your client or your company faced in the story? Explain in "painful" detail how the issue affected everyone involved. This portion of the story is where you want to use words and metaphors that are highly visual, visceral, and evoke emotion.
2. **The Resolution:** Here is where you will guide your prospect through the journey of finding a solution to resolve the conflict. Tell them how you explored various options and the process that you followed to get to the resolution.
3. **The Results:** Be sure to review what happened when the resolution was implemented. Illustrate the effectiveness of what you settled on and the impact on all of the parties involved.

# Training Tip #43: Be Self-Aware

Just like any other valuable sales skill you may employ, self-awareness is also a skill. We often lie to ourselves about the progress we are making on important goals. Why do we do this? Because this is how the brain works. It is a natural human trait to act more out of self-preservation than out of rationality. We have a tendency to tell ourselves tales that justify what we're doing or failing to do. Unfortunately, the tendency is to allow our stories to masquerade as facts. We seek information that reinforces our view and filter out or ignore information that contradicts our view.

For example, if you want to lose weight, you might claim that you're eating healthy, but in reality your eating habits may not have changed very much. You make one modification and blow it up to make it a bigger deal than it really is. Unfortunately, it's usually not enough to get you to your goal. You make soft excuses that make yourself feel better about having a goal that you haven't made much real progress towards. You tell yourself little lies about your progress or your intentions to make yourself feel better.

So why do these little lies matter? They matter because they are preventing you from being self-aware. When you use feel-good statements to track your progress in life, you end up lying to yourself about what you're actually doing. If you are seeking to be a top performer, a peak performer, this behavior will cause you to fall short of what you are trying to achieve. You must have self-awareness before you can achieve self-improvement.

There are a number of tools that you can use to gain "reality" awareness to help you measure, adjust, and gain progress toward your self-improvement goals. One very effective tool that has been used by people for centuries is a journal. A journal can be a great tool for writing down what you plan to do, what you did, and, upon review, how you might modify your behavior to achieve your desired course of action.

Another great tool is annual reflection and review. Many people who use this tool will take anywhere from one to five days, sometimes more, to review notes, journals, planners and other mechanisms that they used to plan and track progress. An annual review often encompasses a mental summary of your core values and personal mission statement. You can also do a personal review over shorter time periods; daily, weekly, monthly, and quarterly.

Probably the most impactful area that you can practice self-awareness in is how you spend your time. If you are like most people in the Western world, you probably spend a fair amount of time online. Gaining a deeper understanding of your behavior online will increase your behavioral awareness, effectiveness, and productivity. One tool that many sales professionals use to monitor their online activities is called RescueTime. This product will completely track your online activities and generate a report that you can review. It runs in the background so it won't interfere with anything you are doing. However, get ready to be surprised when you view your activity report. You are sure to become aware of many things you didn't know—time wasters—and it will allow you to make necessary adjustments.

Getting an accountability partner is another great way to increase your self-awareness. We all have blind spots in our thinking patterns and behaviors. Sharing your goals and ambitions with another person can help to keep you on track. Asking for regular constructive feedback cuts through any self-deceit you might have. Make sure that you ask people who you respect and will tell you what you need to hear, not what you want to hear.

Self-awareness is one of the fundamental aspects of behavior change and is one of the pillars of personal growth. It is very hard to change anything in your life if you aren't measuring what you are doing. Trying to build better habits and sales skills without self-awareness is like firing arrows while you are blindfolded. You can't expect to hit the bullseye if you're not sure where the target is located.

# Training Tip #44: It's Not the Economy, Stupid!

"It's the economy, stupid" was a phrase coined by political strategist James Carnville during the election year that ushered Bill Clinton into the office of U.S. President. Carville's original phrase was meant for internal consumption. It was one of the messages that he wanted the campaign workers to focus on as the then prevailing recession weighed heavy on the minds of Americans. Among others things, this dissatisfaction with the economic recession was one of the issues that enabled Clinton to unseat a one-term sitting president. Blaming the economy might be a good strategy for politics but it is a terrible strategy for the business professional. In fact, it's not even a strategy—it's a poor excuse!

If your sales are lackluster, don't blame the economy, your product or others for your lack of performance. Take full responsibility for your successes or lack of success. The most successful salespeople are high performers in all types of economic situations. They learn how to adjust their approach to match changing competitive or environmental conditions. When you blame your performance on external situations, you are just making an excuse for yourself. When you do this, you deny yourself the opportunity to learn, grow and develop. This behavior slots you into a vicious cycle where you are destined to make the same mistake and suffer the same consequences over and over again.

When will the economy take a downturn? No one can predict when it will happen, but we can predict with 100% accuracy that it will happen. Historical evidence and the cyclical nature of business dictates this to be the case. When the tough economic times come, there are some simple things you can focus on to ensure you don't become a victim or part of the downtrend.

The first thing to do is not let yourself get sucked into the negative talk and thinking. Even when times get tough, there are always qualified prospects who need the goods and services you sell. Though the pace of business may be slower, it still goes on. It is your job to seek them out and engage in a relationship that helps them purchase from you. There will be the losers. Don't let that be you.

What do you think your clients are doing in a tough economy? Many of them are likely in survival mode and looking for ways to thrive. This is your opportunity to provide valuable solutions using your products and services and increase your sales in the process. Always be focused on solving problems for your prospects. Sure, tough economic times can create a mindset of thrift and hoarding of capital resources, but your prospects still have problems they need solved.

The first thing many salespeople and companies do in tough times is adjust their price downwards. This is a mistake! Focus on how you'll be able to help them with their problems and not on lowering your price. Your competitors will be focused on lowering their price, thus positioning themselves as a commodity. They've put themselves in a different category of supplier. Your goal should be to deliver value.

Expand your sales and marketing efforts; don't contract. The natural inclination for companies when tough economic times come is to cut spending in key areas that relate to growing their business. Typically, sales and marketing are areas that are affected. This is counterproductive to the survival of your business. Now, more than ever, is the time you should be focused on doing things to find new customers and expand your business.

What do you think your competitors will be doing during this time? If they think like most companies, they'll be retreating and waiting until the economy improves. But if you expand and multiply your sales and marketing efforts, you have a decent chance of acquiring new customers and new business opportunities, maybe even some of your competitors' customers.

# Training Tip #45: Early to Bed Early to Rise

Every athlete knows the importance that rest can have on the body and its ability to perform at peak levels. The same holds true in business. Ben Franklin said it best: "Early to bed early to rise makes a man healthy, wealthy, and wise." The right amount of sleep is critical to performing at the top of your game whether it be in athletics or in business.

In 1942, 8 hours of sleep was the norm, now 6.8 is the average amount of sleep that people get. Twenty percent of the world's population is sleep deprived. In the United States, the number is close to 35%. How can getting the right amount of sleep help you in sales? The simple answer is that if you do get the proper amount of sleep for your body you're already way ahead of the people who don't.

Unfortunately, in many frenzied corporate cultures, sleeplessness is confused with vitality and high performance. In fact, the truth is quite the opposite. Companies have rules about drug and alcohol use, smoking, and sexual harassment, but none have prescriptive rules that advise against overwork at the expense of sleep. In fact, there's no difference between driving drunk and driving while sleep deprived. However you carve it, it's called driving while impaired. So if sleep deprivation manifests itself in the body the same as drug impairment, how effective are those sleep deprived business professionals?

How is getting the right amount of sleep important to your sales success? Ask yourself this question. Who would you rather do business with, someone who looked tired, worn, with low energy, without an enthusiastic look of their face or someone with an energetic, healthy, and happy demeanor? Of course the answer is the latter. In a recent U.S. presidential election, one of the candidates had disparaging nicknames for many of his opponents. And, sadly, the only thing many people will remember about "Low Energy Jeb" was his nickname instead of the many contributions that he made as a civil servant. So don't discount your appearance when it comes to the type of vitality that comes from proper rest and recovery.

Enthusiasm sells. If don't have it you have the opposite. And your prospect will look for ways to get you out of their office so that you don't rub off on them. If you are tired, you'll likely not present yourself in the most enthusiastic manner.

Your emotional state is not the only thing affected by lack of proper sleep. Your cognitive functions can suffer as well. If you stay awake longer than 18 consecutive hours your mind will not operate at peak performance. Your reaction speed, your ability to focus, your ability to learn, and your decision-making capacity all start to suffer. Another negative aspect of sleep deprivation is increased appetite. Sleep deprivation interrupts the natural regulation of hunger hormones causing your appetite to increase. People often crave fatty, unhealthy foods resulting in increased weight gain and other physical maladies.

If you are sleep deprived over a number of days, the result is the same as one consecutive run of staying awake. But if you manage to get a minimum of eight hours of sleep each night, your level of alertness should remain stable throughout the day. The amount of sleep needed is different for every individual. Know your ideal sleep hours (6, 7, 8, 9 or more) and incorporate them into your life.

Starting the day early is another success principle. You'll find that most peak performers get a head start on those who are mediocre performers. Research shows that your brain function is at its peak 2–3 hours after you wake up. Your creativity and your ability to think at your highest cognitive levels are the greatest during this time period. So, how do you spend those first few hours of the day?

# Training Tip #46: Know the Buying Roles

Make sure you know the roles of all the people you are dealing with. Your ultimate goal is to get to the person who can make a decision, sign a contract or authorize payment. You should identify that person early in the process and look for ways to engage them.

Sometimes there is not a direct path to the decision maker. You'll have to navigate the organization to determine the different types of people who can help lead you to your end goal, the sale. Along the way, never forget that all the people you interact with and who play a role in the sales process are important. Treat them ALL with respect and appreciation. You'll encounter many different types of people in the sales cycle. They mostly break down into four groups, which are: 1) The Initiator, 2) The Influencer, 3) The User, and 4) The Buyer.

Often, in larger organizations, there are individuals responsible for identifying resources or gathering information that can help their company to make a purchase. These people are "The Initiators". Though this individual is usually not responsible for making a decision, the manner in which they present their findings can "slant" the eventual purchase decision in your favor or against you.

Remember that you are the industry expert. Help prospects by providing all the knowledge and information you can to assist them in completing their job. Your company's products are probably only a small piece of what they are responsible for. They'll appreciate that you've gone beyond just your own product to help.

Another key person in the sale process is "The Influencer". This person is internal to the organization and is the person who tries to convince others that they need the product. Typically, this individual is someone who understands the internal problem and how your product can solve the problem. They can also be an extension of your sales efforts.

There can be many influencers in an organization. One of the challenges is to ensure that the person who favors your product and is trying to influence others to accept it is respected in their own organization. Sadly, many sales have been lost because the influencer either lacked credibility or their recommendations were questioned due to internal politics.

"The User" also can play an important role. If this is someone who will use your product or service they need to be educated about why your solution will make their life better. If this doesn't occur, they might become an impediment to the sale if they are not convinced that a change will benefit them. And then they become the negative influencer.

Another thing to think about is the user's influence after the sale has been made. If you are selling a product or service or some type of continuity contract, their satisfaction may be critical to your renewal. If they were not sold in the first place, they may undermine your efforts when the contract comes up for renewal. The buyer will realize that the product or service is not being used or supported by the organization and your chances to close the sale again diminish significantly.

Finally, the last type of person in the organization is "The Buyer". This person is the individual who makes the final decision on the purchase. Typically, this person will follow a process that quantifies the various choices and leads to a final decision. It is not uncommon for this individual to also be the initiator. In these instances, your ability to make a connection is extremely important.

The establishment of trust and credibility is sometimes all the Buyer needs to choose you as the preferred vendor. Once they've made this decision, they will go through a process of justifying it using the facts and information that you provide them. In the field of psychology, this is known as the emotive-cognitive sales process and it drives every purchase decision.

# Training Tip #47: Selling Is Not Convincing

You can't make people buy and if you pressure them into a sale you will regret it. Dale Carnegie in his famous book *How to Win Friends and Influence People* said, "A man convinced against his will is of the same opinion still." Sales is all about sharing information, building a trust relationship, and finding ways to deliver value to your prospect. It's about solving problems and leaving your customer in a better place than when you first encountered them.

Sales is not about convincing. It's about influencing. Of course you are going to share information about your product or service, but how you share that information is critical. If you are not open to presenting your product in a manner that is conducive to solving the customer's problem you will not make a connection. You can only influence if you can make a connection with your prospect, and understanding and speaking the prospect's language is the way to do that.

There are three fundamental principles about language that can help a salesperson have greater influence. First, every customer speaks in his or her own unique language. Many companies provide their salespeople with a "one size fits all" company sales pitch. Here's the problem with that. Each person on this planet speaks his or her own unique language. And if they don't speak "your company language" you will never connect with them.

Their language is devised by all the experiences in their life; where they grew up, the language used by their family, where they went to school, their friends, the people they work with, etc. Therefore, the language two people use to describe the same situation may be very different.

So what do you do to bridge the communication gap? You work to build "rapport" through harmonized communication. This harmonization can only occur if you speak your prospect or customer's language. But if you don't know their language you can't do that. Here's the secret. Their language is all about them. Most salespeople talk about themselves, their product or their pitch. People don't care about what you have to say until they know you care about them.

In order for you to learn their language you'll have to do some listening. You'll have to learn about the things they care about. Successful salespeople talk the language of their prospects by knowing them as people. They talk about their problems, their values, and their plans and desires. Do this and you'll build rapport.

Communication is also not just about the words you use. An immense amount of information is conveyed non-verbally as well. This means that the successful sales professional will adapt their mental wiring and language to mirror that of their customer. This is a bit trickier and really is an art that must be developed over time. You have to be careful not to mimic your customer's every move. This is a newbie mistake and it will backfire … so be careful.

Influence is the process of projecting your beliefs and convictions on to another human being. It's not about convincing them to agree with you or accept your business case or sales proposal. Influence is about making them internalize your message.

The most effective way to do this is to make them smarter and give them an edge on their competition. Once they believe that the information you are sharing with them is in their best interests, they will internalize it and you have begun the process of building trust and influence. Finally, do not "pretend" to care. You should be genuine. If you don't genuinely care about people you will not succeed in sales.

# Training Tip #48: Trust Trumps Skill

The trust that a customer has in your company and in you strongly outweighs the techniques you use to sell. Building trust is better than any sales technique. It really is all about the relationship. Time and time again it has been shown that a person with an inferior product can win the sale over a superior product if they have developed a strong bond, a strong, trusted relationship with the prospect.

It sometimes can take years to build trust and that trust can be broken in a matter of seconds. This is why it is important to act in a credible and honest manner. Benjamin Franklin said, "Half the truth is often a whole lie." You may think it clever to withhold a piece of information from your client or prospect. If you didn't say anything you weren't lying, right? Perhaps your mouth didn't speak the words, but your heart did.

The best salespeople are honest. They build trust and do nothing intentionally to breach that trust. They own up to mistakes that they make and do not blame others. They acknowledge lapses right away and take immediate steps to rectify the situation. Trust is the glue that holds together the buyer-seller relationship. Without trust, you will not be successful in business or in life.

Here are three ways that you can create a trusted relationship. The first way is to create an emotional connection. The most important thing is to be yourself. Don't play games or act in any other manner that is not you because you think that might influence the customer. Unless you are a professional actor you won't succeed … and you won't be trusted. Build a personal brand based on honesty and integrity. Be authentic. Too many salespeople worry about being perfect in their presentations. Believe it or not, most people won't trust you if you appear to be "too slick". They want to know that you are human like them.

Develop a reputation for being trustworthy and honest in your communications and your actions. Focus on your customers' success, not your success of selling them. Take the time to understand your customers' needs and their situation. When you do this, you are making an effort to see the world through their eyes and this will go a long way toward building trust in your relationship with them.

Don't be afraid to let the customer or prospect know a little about you. This should come naturally in the back and forth dialogue as you're getting to know them. You'll want to find experiences that are shared and that can begin to build the emotional connection.

The second method that you'll want to employ is to know the impact your product or service can make on the prospect. This can only come from doing your homework and really understanding the prospect's business. Ideally, you've done a lot of research prior to ever having that very first meeting. Your ability to share your point of view on potential solutions is a key factor in building trust. This also speaks to your ability to present yourself as an expert on what you are selling. Because if you are not, why do they need you?

In summary, integrity is everything. Always do the right thing and demonstrate that you have moral principles. Honor your commitments. Do what you promise and do it well.

# Training Tip #49: Never Accept Good

Never accept good enough as good enough. Always push yourself harder than others would ever dare. Having a mindset of continuous improvement will create opportunities that can put you in that top 5% in your field.

What is good enough? Is there a standard by which "good enough" can be determined or measured? Of course not. The problem is that one person's "good enough" might be another person's failure. However, when you set your standards very high, even your flaws might be viewed as excellent. And, if you want to be in that top 5%, excellent should be your new standard.

Going from good to excellent is a mindset. It takes a conscious effort to make a self-analysis and put together a plan to strive for excellence. The pursuit of excellence should not be confused with an obsession with perfectionism.

Excellence is the very opposite of perfectionism. Perfectionism is losing your true self in pursuit of a standard that can never be obtained. Excellence, on the other hand, is the pursuit of continuous improvement, striving to look for betterment in all that you do.

The good thing about striving for excellence is that it is not hard to get started. There is no high bar that if not met means you fail. It was W. Edwards Deming who said that, "organizations must have a consistency of purpose and a dedication to constant, ongoing improvement in order to satisfy customers, beat the competition, and retain jobs."

Striving for excellence is continuous improvement and the measurement is as simple as being better in whatever you do than the last time you did it. It's as simple as just getting started and measuring what you do, improving your performance, then measuring again.

Here are some things to help you get there:

- Always give more than what is expected of you. Look for ways that you can deliver greater value in everything you do. Don't under promise and over deliver. Promise and over deliver!
- Challenge yourself to improve in everything you do. Small, incremental changes are easier than big changes and are the best way to accomplish this. Remember that the sum of the parts is greater than the whole.
- Be passionate about what you do. If you hate your company, your coworkers, your boss or your job it's time to make a change. You're cheating yourself and everyone else who counts on you because you will never deliver your best in this type of situation. Find a situation that you can be passionate about and give all that you can.
- Always follow through and follow up (see Tip #26). Finish what you start and deliver on your promises.
- Be a student of your experiences and the experiences of others. Learn from your mistakes to improve your performance. Remember that only wisdom can be gained by experience, good and bad. Take all that wisdom and incorporate it into your self-improvement plan.

Pick two or three of these areas to focus on and you'll begin to see big differences in your success. Other people will notice the difference too.

# Training Tip #50: Get a Coach or Mentor

If you want to really grow, invest in a professional business coach. A business coach is somebody who helps you move from where you are to where you want to be. The coach does this by focusing solely on your goals. A good coach can help take you places in your career that you might not have thought possible. All of the top successful sales professionals have a coach or mentor.

It is a great time to live in. The information available to the sales professional is expansive. There is a plethora of websites, companies, and online resources available for the sales professional to sharpen their skills. Processes and formulas that are tried and true make much of this a science. If you follow the formula you get the desired results.

Here's the challenge. There's so much information available that it can be like drinking from a firehose. The challenge is not only to absorb the information and make it part of who you are but to also make sure it is the correct information to begin with! This is where the real value of a business coach can come into play. Most sales professionals don't want to spend years and years learning new techniques and finding out which ones work best for them. Time is money!

A good business coach can assist the sales professional in advising on the right information and skills to incorporate into their professional lives. The typical business coach will read 50–100 books a year, minimally attend at least four seminars a year, and spend tens of thousands of dollars annually on coaching and training for themselves.

When you hire a coach, you get the benefit of all this knowledge and training! Your business coach can sort through all this acquired knowledge and impart the information, skills, and tactics that are best for your particular situation.

Another benefit a business coach can bring to the sales professional is providing someone to bounce ideas off of. The coach will act as a sounding board and will use a series of non-judgmental questioning to draw out additional information valuable to the ideation process. These types of interactions can also help the person being coached to expand awareness and make and implement better decisions.

Coaches are also great accountability partners. A business coach can challenge and assist you in developing smart goals and strategies to help you achieve those goals and hold you accountable to the process. They can help hold you accountable to follow through with your goals and help you get creative and try new strategies to move to your next level when you are stuck. They can also help you identify the habits and thoughts that are sabotaging your success and provide insights into replacing those habits with improved ones that increase your level of success.

An experienced coach not only challenges your thinking and willingness to grow but they can also act as someone who has "been there and done that". Their knowledge and experience can provide unique insights that will allow you to avoid career pitfalls while also broadening your business awareness. Think of a business coach as a trusted advisor who'll work with you to identify your strengths, help you set achievable goals, and motivate you to make the very best of your business.

Finally, where the rubber meets the road for the sales professional is revenue. Price Waterhouse Coopers found that the return of investment (ROI) for coaching was 7 times the initial investment and another study found that over 25% of coaching clients reported ROI in the range of 10 to 49 times! Where else can you make an investment, get a coach, mentor, trusted advisor and make a massive return on your investment?

# Are You an IronMan Mind Sales Professional?

So now you've been through all 50 training tips. Some may have been new to you and there were probably many you knew about already. The big question is how many of these training tips do you currently implement into your sales practice? Take the test below and see how you score.

Do you have your own personal brand?
\_\_\_\_ No (0 points) \_\_\_\_ Sort of (1 point) \_\_\_\_ Yes (3 points)

Do you ask every client for a testimonial?
\_\_\_\_ No (0 points) \_\_\_\_ Sort of (1 point) \_\_\_\_ Yes (3 points)

Do you use social media for your business 3 or more times a week?
\_\_\_\_ No (0 points) \_\_\_\_ Sometimes (1 point) \_\_\_\_ Yes (3 points)

Do you use referral marketing techniques to acquire leads?
\_\_\_\_ No (0 points) \_\_\_\_ Sort of (1 point) \_\_\_\_ Yes (3 points)

Do you build your sales funnel daily?
\_\_\_\_ No (0 points) \_\_\_\_ Sort of (1 point) \_\_\_\_ Yes (3 points)

Do you stay in regularly scheduled contact with all of your clients?
\_\_\_\_ No (0 points) \_\_\_\_ Sort of (1 point) \_\_\_\_ Yes (3 points)

Do you use CRM software to manage your daily schedule and task list?
\_\_\_\_ No (0 points) \_\_\_\_ Sort of (1 point) \_\_\_\_ Yes (3 points)

Do you focus on the most important things every day?
\_\_\_\_ No (0 points) \_\_\_\_ Sort of (1 point) \_\_\_\_ Yes (3 points)

Do you regularly update your sales pitch?
\_\_\_\_ No (0 points) \_\_\_\_ Sort of (1 point) \_\_\_\_ Yes (3 points)

Do you use a set of techniques to motivate yourself daily?
\_\_\_\_ No (0 points) \_\_\_\_ Sort of (1 point) \_\_\_\_ Yes (3 points)

Do you regularly analyze your performance to see if you are meeting your set goals and objectives?
\_\_\_\_ No (0 points) \_\_\_\_ Sort of (1 point) \_\_\_\_ Yes (3 points)

Do you have a written personal development plan?
\_\_\_\_ No (0 points) \_\_\_\_ Sort of (1 point) \_\_\_\_ Yes (3 points)

Do you regularly attend industry events (more than 3 times a year)?
\_\_\_\_ No (0 points) \_\_\_\_ Sort of (1 point) \_\_\_\_ Yes (3 points)

Do you regularly network to get new prospects?
\_\_\_\_ No (0 points) \_\_\_\_ Sort of (1 point) \_\_\_\_ Yes (3 points)

Have you created your own Meetup or Tweetup?
\_\_\_\_ No (0 points) \_\_\_\_ Thinking about it (1 point) \_\_\_\_ Yes (3 points)

Do you create your own industry-relevant media like a blog, vlog or podcast?
\_\_\_\_ No (0 points) \_\_\_\_ Thinking about it (1 point) \_\_\_\_ Yes (3 points)

Are you purposely learning something new every day?
\_\_\_\_ No (0 points) \_\_\_\_ Sort of (1 point) \_\_\_\_ Yes (3 points)

Do you monitor your competitors' websites and newsfeeds?
\_\_\_\_ No (0 points) \_\_\_\_ Sort of (1 point) \_\_\_\_ Yes (3 points)

Do you find ways to raise the price of your product/service or create packages to increase the total customer investment?
\_\_\_\_ No (0 points) \_\_\_\_ Sort of (1 point) \_\_\_\_ Yes (3 points)

Do you use the concept of scarcity to influence your prospect/customer to make a purchase?
\_\_\_\_ No (0 points) \_\_\_\_ Thinking about it (1 point) \_\_\_\_ Yes (3 points)

Do you create a written daily plan that you follow?
\_\_\_\_ No (0 points) \_\_\_\_ Sort of (1 point) \_\_\_\_ Yes (3 points)

Do you create vendor partnerships or cross sell sales scenarios to add value for your prospect/customers?
_____ No (0 points) _____ Sort of (1 point) _____ Yes (3 points)

Do you create educational seminars for your prospects/clients?
_____ No (0 points) _____ Thinking of it (1 point) _____ Yes (3 points)

Do you have a written "why"?
_____ No (0 points) _____ Sort of (1 point) _____ Yes (3 points)

Do you follow up immediately after a prospect/customer call?
_____ No (0 points) _____ Sort of (1 point) _____ Yes (3 points)

Do you know how to achieve balance between your work and personal life?
_____ No (0 points) _____ Sort of (1 point) _____ Yes (3 points)

Do you have an avatar of your ideal customer that you target?
_____ No (0 points) _____ Sort of (1 point) _____ Yes (3 points)

Do you follow a formalized sales process?
_____ No (0 points) _____ Sort of (1 point) _____ Yes (3 points)

Do you preplan your sales calls?
_____ No (0 points) _____ Sort of (1 point) _____ Yes (3 points)

Do you leave every sales call with agreed upon next steps?
_____ No (0 points) _____ Sometimes (1 point) _____ Yes (3 points)

Do you practice for your sales presentations 1 hour for each minute of the presentation?
_____ No (0 points) _____ Sort of (1 point) _____ Yes (3 points)

Do you actively work to put out positive energy when you are alone or with other people?
_____ No (0 points) _____ Sort of (1 point) _____ Yes (3 points)

Do you follow a call script when you make cold calls?
_____ No (0 points) _____ Sometimes (1 point) _____ Yes (3 points)

Do you analyze your non-successes and modify your behavior to change the outcome?
\_\_\_\_ No (0 points) \_\_\_\_ Sort of (1 point) \_\_\_\_ Yes (3 points)

Do you regularly read/listen to books in order to increase your knowledge and skills?
\_\_\_\_ No (0 points) \_\_\_\_ Sometimes (1 point) \_\_\_ Yes (3 points)

Do you use your downtime to be more productive?
\_\_\_\_ No (0 points) \_\_\_\_ Sort of (1 point) \_\_\_\_ Yes (3 points)

Do you offer an upsell when you make a sales presentation?
\_\_\_\_ No (0 points) \_\_\_\_ Sometimes (1 point) \_\_\_ Yes (3 points)

Do you know all about your customers' customer?
\_\_\_\_ No (0 points) \_\_\_\_ Sort of (1 point) \_\_\_\_ Yes (3 points)

Do you believe that it is not the economy, the competition, your product or price that is responsible for your success?
\_\_\_\_ No (0 points) \_\_\_\_ Sort of (1 point) \_\_\_\_ Yes (3 points)

Do you get the right amount of sleep every night for your body type?
\_\_\_\_ No (0 points) \_\_\_\_ Sort of (1 point) \_\_\_\_ Yes (3 points)

Do you always know who the decision maker is at your prospect?
\_\_\_\_ No (0 points) \_\_\_\_ Sort of (1 point) \_\_\_\_ Yes (3 points)

Do you consciously use "influence" techniques with your prospects/customers?
\_\_\_\_ No (0 points) \_\_\_\_ Sort of (1 point) \_\_\_\_ Yes (3 points)

Do you consciously do things to build trust with your prospect/customer?
\_\_\_\_ No (0 points) \_\_\_\_ Sort of (1 point) \_\_\_\_ Yes (3 points)

Do you continually analyze your performance and look for ways to improve?
\_\_\_\_ No (0 points) \_\_\_\_ Sort of (1 point) \_\_\_\_ Yes (3 points)

Do you have a sales coach, business coach or mentor?

\_\_\_\_ No (0 points) \_\_\_\_ Sort of (1 point) \_\_\_\_ Yes (3 points)

YOUR SCORE:

121 - 135: You need to be coaching/teaching this material.

108 - 120: You are an IronMan Mind Sales Professional.

94 - 107: You are pretty good at this.

81 - 93: You are barely passing.

80 or less: Time to get some training.

No matter the results of your score, even the most experienced professionals are looking for ways to increase their sales effectiveness. For more sales training resources, take a look at the resources in the pages that follow. You can also take the test online and get a more detailed assessment, developmental recommendations, and offers related specifically to your skill ranking.

**Go to: www.TheIronManMind.com/Sales-Skills-Assessment**

## Bonus Sales Training

**Are you ready for more great content and sales strategies?**

Congratulations on getting to the end of this book. You're now armed with 50 powerful sales training tips and 10 powerful mind principles. It is said that "knowledge is power." But the truth is applied knowledge is power. To help you apply your new-found knowledge, you've been granted free access to additional resources that can help you integrate these techniques into your daily practice. This information will help you to:

- Utilize a proven methodology to consistently plan for a successful outcome with each sales call
- Create warm and engaging connections with both new and existing customers
- Skillfully use the right mix of questions and active listening to promote a robust dialogue with customers to discover their needs
- Recognize opportunities to close and demonstrate confidence in asking for the business

Go ahead and sign up for free:<br/>
www.SalesTrainingResource.com

# IronMan Mind Sales Success Training Camp

Are you ready to take your sales success to the next level? The key to progress in any endeavor in life is taking action. The more focused action you can take the greater the result you will see. To help you put the knowledge you've acquired into action, *The IronMan Mind Success Training Camp* has been developed for you to continue your professional growth.

*The IronMan Sales Success Training Camp* is a 50-week program that follows Dr. Richard Greene's book, *The IronMan Sales Success Formula,* and provides an in-depth approach to significantly increase revenues and profits in your business. In this program, Dr. Greene will lead you through each training tip with greater detail and examples of how to effectively integrate these tips into your sales practice.

**Program Description:**
*The IronMan Mind Sales Success Training Camp* is for the sales professional or business owner who wants to increase their successes in both business and in their personal life. This 50-week program focuses on key areas that will propel you to greater levels of sales success and profitability. It doesn't matter where you are starting from, this program will benefit both new and seasoned sales professional.

By applying any combination of just a few strategies, you will begin to notice a difference almost immediately as you absorb the knowledge you'll learn, work the exercises, and apply these principles to your business. Facilitated by *Dr. Richard Greene, The IronMan Business Coach*, you'll be presented with strategies and tactics that will really make a difference in your business.

**This isn't just theory**. With over 30 years of experience in the corporate world, Dr. Greene teaches principals that thousands of sales professionals have employed in real-world business and sales environments. They are tried and tested and most every successful sales professional uses the principles taught in this program.

## How it Works:

*The IronMan Mind Sales Success Training Camp* is a training course that is created to be flexible for busy people. Successful people don't have time to waste and they need the ability to create success in a manner that is doesn't conflict with their busy lives. This means that you can comfortably expand your knowledge and skills around your existing work and family commitments.

Subject materials are <u>delivered weekly</u> for 50-weeks via audio, video, and text so you can choose which best fits your learning style. You'll get the critical information presented to you along with a personal set of lessons used to support the information and to create a transformational change in your sales career.

To increase the effectiveness of the program, you'll be able to connect to live Q&A calls monthly where you can get answers specific to your particular situation. You'll also be eligible to join the members-only Facebook group where you get additional content and support from other top sales professionals. As an added bonus, all *IronMan Mind Sales Success Training Camp* members get a 30-minute personal Strategy Session with Dr. Richard Greene.

## Enrollment Process:

Taking the step to invest in yourself is one of the best decisions you can make. You just need to make the decision to be committed to continue to learn and grow in your profession. As a member of the program you'll get access to:

- 50 weeks of powerful video & audio learning materials
- A members-only Facebook group
- Live monthly live Q&A for 50 straight weeks
- A 30-minute 1:1 strategic coaching session with Dr. Greene

**More details at: www.IronManSalesTraining.com**

# About the Author

**Dr. Richard B. Greene, DBA, SSBB, CMPE**
**Speaker, Author, IronMan Mind Business Coach**

Dr. Greene's experience spans more than 30 years as a corporate sales executive across many different industries. He's an author, a business coach, and entrepreneur. Over the course of his career, he's had the opportunity to work with some of the world's brightest minds in business and commerce.

As a researcher in the field of human potential, he's studied the success factors of those who are the top in their industries and developed systems that professionals use to create unparalleled success in their careers and in their lives. Dr. Greene developed his success philosophy early in his professional career when he discovered the power of effective time management.

Rich is an advocate for the application of "process" to achieve super productivity. Traditional processes provide a formula and order of activities an individual must take to go from point A to point B. They'll contain detailed tactics and contingency plans in the event of plan deviation. But the best plan is not a guarantee of success. Rich observed that having talent and skills also did not guarantee success. **The missing ingredient is a mindset that is creative, powerful, and unstoppable.**

Over the years, Rich has employed many popular strategies to create a mindset that contributed to his success. However, it was when working as a Masters Swim Coach helping triathletes to prepare for their Ironman races where that he discovered that these athletes had a unique way of thinking about success. This mindset was so powerful that it enabled these athletes to face extreme challenges and succeed where most other people would fail.

After years of research working with Ironman triathletes to understand this special mind power, Dr. Greene has captured this unique mind ability and incorporated it into an elite executive training program called the *IronMan Mind*. Applied properly, the IronMan Mind techniques can transform your mind into a powerful tool that, combined with the right skill sets, can make your success unstoppable.

Dr. Greene is the founder of ***Amplifier***, a business coaching and consulting company located in Sacramento, California. He works with executives in the U.S. and internationally and is also an active Ironman triathlete and marathon swimmer.

To contact Rich, go to his website www.IronManBusinessCoach.com or send him a letter to:

Amplifier, LLC
Post Street, #5304
El Dorado Hills, California 95762

# Other Book Titles by Richard B. Greene

 The 10 Commandments of Peak Performance

 The 10 Commandments of Productive Meetings

 The Science of Using Affirmations and Attraction Strategies to Get Everything You Want in Life

 The IronMan Mind Book of Quotes: Inspirational Quotes for Winners

You can find these books and other powerful Peak Performance development products at www.AmplifyYourResults.com

Made in the USA
San Bernardino, CA
20 May 2018